PERSONALITY QUIZZES

Dr. Dorothy McCoy, M.A., Ph.D.

Publications International, Ltd.

Dr. Dorothy McCoy, M.A., Ph.D., is an author, speaker, instructor, and psychotherapist who was in private practice for 15 years. Dr. McCoy has a Bachelor of Arts degree from the University of South Carolina, a Masters in Clinical Counseling from the Citadel, and a Doctorate in Counseling Psychology from the University of Sarasota. She is a member of the Society for Police and Criminal Psychology, the American Academy of Experts in Traumatic Stress, and the Public Safety Leadership Consortium. She is the author of *From Shyness to Social Butterfly*, *The Ultimate Book of Personality Tests*, *Your Ultimate Quiz: 500 Fun and Fascinating Questions*, and *The Manipulative Man*.

Image credits: Art Explosion; Digital Vision; PhotoDisc; Shutterstock; Stockbyte

ISBN-13: 978-1-4127-7794-0
ISBN-10: 1-4127-7794-1

Manufactured in China.

8 7 6 5 4 3 2 1

Contents

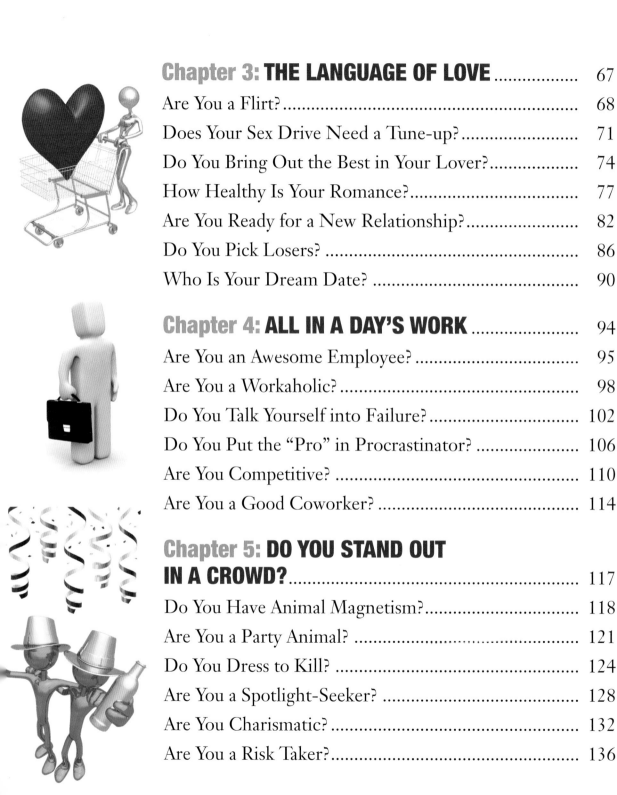

GETTING TO KNOW YOU
GETTING TO KNOW ALL ABOUT YOU

Although each of us is wonderfully unique, we are also marvelously connected to everyone around us. The quizzes in this book will help you learn about your uniqueness as well as your connection to all the people who make

up your social, career, and family circles—and, actually, believe it or not, to all of humankind.

Yes, the quizzes are fun to take and a snap to score, and they also offer valuable insights. They will help you explore your general personality traits and open up new areas for you to examine and embrace. And they'll provide plenty of fun, laughter, and room for introspection along the way! Real-life, relatable scenarios make each quiz relevant and useful.

How Do I Score the Quizzes?

Good news! There are no "right" or "wrong" answers to these questions, just as there are no "good" or "bad" personalities. All types of people are needed to make the world go 'round. The

organized personalities help keep the creative folks on track. The fun-lovers help the rest of us remember to whistle while we work.

Timing Is Important

Your outlook and your mood at the time you take a quiz may influence your score. For example, taking the "optimism" quiz after you've just been promoted at work or when you're at the start of an exciting new relationship would likely result in a very different score than if you were to take it when you'd just quarreled with your sweetie or lost an important account. Additionally, taking a quiz five years from now, after you have matured, experienced more of life, and evolved as a person, would likely produce a different result than what you would tally today. So keep in mind that while these quizzes are good indicators of your personality traits, they are not "the gospel." If you decide you want to make changes in your life, we have scattered suggestions for positive growth throughout the book.

Circular Relationships

The quizzes are loosely divided into seven sections that are representative of several essential areas of your life. Your thoughts

and behaviors, valuable relationships, romantic life, career or vocation, and areas of fun combine to create your unique world. As you spend time in each section you will notice that one quiz can flow naturally into another,

just as one personality trait can blend into or complement another trait. Optimism probably influences sense of humor, which may impact popularity. Self-confidence is directly linked to how you see yourself, your level of charisma, and whether you feel comfortable taking risks. All of our traits are interconnected in one way or another.

Your Personal Journey

Enjoy exploring your hidden talents and strengths and discovering the secrets of relationships and strong bonds. Nothing can be more valuable than learning about yourself. Success is no more than understanding who you are and in what areas you excel, and learning to embrace what makes you *you*.

CHAPTER 1

ALL ABOUT YOU

There are certain characteristics that go to the heart of who you are as a human being: your thoughts, behaviors, preferences, and propensities. Your right brain/left brain dominance affects how you see and interpret the world. Knowing your intelligence style is crucial as well, because your style of intelligence will explain much about you and your unique abilities.

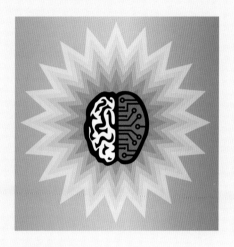

Your dreams are the portal into your inner world; what do yours say about you? Find out how to gauge your emotional maturity, which can affect your wellness, your relationships, and your career. What about your great sense of humor? A good sense of humor is an immensely valuable social characteristic—and fun, to boot. Are you intuitive? Do you see beyond the obvious? Learn how your intuition quotient affects your life.

As you take these quizzes, you'll get to the heart of what really makes you tick.

Tell Me, Who Are You?

By our very nature, we are social creatures who depend on each other to lend a hand. Therefore, it is reasonable that we value human warmth above most other characteristics. If someone is "warm," it stands to reason that person is also caring, supportive, and will have our back when times are tough.

We turn to warm people for support and to share the good times. The thinkers among us help to organize and structure our lives, and the experience seekers can save the day when we face challenges.

THREE PERSONALITY TYPES

The three general personality types based on this theory are **Cognitive Personality** (seen as less warm), **Emotive Personality** (warm), and **Experience Seeker** (warm or cool—they shift). We tend to form attachments to thoughtful, nurturing emotive types, ask for guidance from cognitive folks, and call on the experience seekers when things turn nasty. Getting to know the cognitive personalities and experience seekers may require some time and effort, but that doesn't mean it's not worth it. There are no right or wrong personality types. We are all needed for our unique contributions.

three-for-all

Everyone is a combination of all three personality types, but the mixture and degree differ from person to person. At work you may be cognitive, at home your caring for your loved ones may shine through, and when you want to be adventuresome the hidden experience seeker in you may show itself.

Tell Me, Who Are You?

Can you roll with the punches?
. . . .

On a scale of 1 to 5, with 1 being the least like you and 5 being the most, how much do the responses to the following situations reflect your attitude?

1. I enjoy nonfiction. 1 2 3 4 5

2. I have been accused (frequently) of not paying attention to what my significant other is saying. 1 2 3 4 5

3. I take great pride in being rational and logical. 1 2 3 4 5

4. I am exhausted by social events. 1 2 3 4 5

5. I am an expert in at least one area. 1 2 3 4 5

6. I cry at sad movies. 1 2 3 4 5

7. I am the person who always remembers to send a greeting card (or feels guilty if I forget). 1 2 3 4 5

8. I am a true candlelight-loving romantic. 1 2 3 4 5

9. "About right" is good enough for me most of the time. 1 2 3 4 5

10. I have a wide (and ever expanding) circle of friends. 1 2 3 4 5

11. As a child, I was the one yelling, "Lookit me, Ma, no hands!" 1 2 3 4 5

12. In sports, I play to win. 1 2 3 4 5

13. I am a problem solver. 1 2 3 4 5

14. I frequently feel bored and restless. 1 2 3 4 5

15. I am in a risky occupation (or would like to be). 1 2 3 4 5

Tell Me, Who Are You?

Summary

Tally up your points in sections: questions 1–5; 6–10; and 11–15. If you tallied 20 or more points in any one section, that is likely your predominant personality trait. If you topped 20 in more than one section, you have dominant traits of more than one type.

20+ points in questions 1–5
Cognitive Personality Type

If you had 20 or more points in this section, you are probably contemplative, perceptive, intelligent, and analytical; perhaps a scientist, technology expert, or physician. Cognitive people usually think rationally, create options, and solve problems. They are valuable resources in any society.

Their priorities may be more career-oriented than people-oriented. This does not mean they love less well; they simply may not show their love in the "usual" ways. For this reason, they may be perceived as less warm than others, or at least slightly chilled.

20+ points in questions 6–10
Emotive Personality Type

Scoring 20 or more points in this section means you are probably a people person. Emotive personality types tend to enjoy being around others and are energized by social situations. They may be quite intelligent and successful, but their defining characteristic is their warm regard for humankind. They are our social workers, therapists, and helpful sales professionals.

Emotive types may not choose to rock their career worlds (although they can if they want to), yet they are usually quite popular and well-loved. They will remember important anniversaries and mark special occasions.

20+ points in questions 11–15
Experience Seeker

You are likely an experience seeker if you scored 20 or above in this section. People call on experience seekers when the wolf is at the door and the lock is giving. They are not always perceived as warm; they will generally show warm or chilled traits depending on the situation. If something must be done—for example, someone must run into a fiery building—call an experience seeker. Cognitive people will tell you it's illogical to run into the building; emotive people will empathize with you when you come out. Experience seekers will race into the inferno with a plan in place and emerge covered in soot—yet alive and well.

They are likely to be in active, sometimes risky professions such as firefighting, law enforcement, the military, or other occupations where tough decisions and decisive action are needed.

Are You Real?

Do you journey though life using your own personal navigation system, or are you too concerned about what you should do or be? Do you worry about what others think of you or your behavior? Are you easily led, or do you lead the way—not caring if others follow? It isn't easy to follow your own star, and it is frequently painful to break with tradition. How can you tell if you are authentic (real) or not?

As a species we seem to prefer people who follow the crowd and obey the cultural rules of society. In prehistoric times, this trait probably helped the tribe stay alive. In modern-day society, however, it's okay to step out of the group and be who you are—if you dare.

Although there may be penalties for roaming unique and free, you may have found that standing tall and saying "Yep, that's me" is worth the price. Your career, your love life, your own personal style, your principles and ethics—these things together are what tells us who we are and makes each of us unique. It's important to find a balance between our place in society and being true to who we are.

Reach down deep inside and pull forth the shining, genuine you. Others will recognize it, smile, and seek your company.

Are You Real?

How much socialization has stuck to you?

1. Are you easily embarrassed?

Yes   No

2. Do people say you are very cooperative?

Yes   No

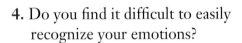

3. Do you seek advice before you make decisions?

Yes   No

4. Do you find it difficult to easily recognize your emotions?

Yes   No

5. Do your strengths and weaknesses seem a little fuzzy and hard to identify?

Yes   No

6. Do you cave in to criticism?

Yes   No

7. Do you feel compelled to dress according to the current style?

Yes   No

8. Is your self-confidence a little shaky?

Yes   No

9. Do you have a lackadaisical sense of purpose and goals?

Yes   No

10. Do you frequently feel conflicting emotions?

Yes   No

| **Are You Real?** |

Scoring

Tally up your "no" answers, giving yourself **1 point** for each, and look for your profile below.

0–4 points
Socially Oriented

You are a people person: traditional and society-oriented. You are still discovering yourself. This is neither good nor bad—it simply is. You may want to become more aware of your individual desires and needs, and you can do this by asking yourself what you get pleasure from. Begin doing those things! Eat what you like, dress in your own personal style, take up a hobby you love, and commit to a job that you look forward to doing. You'll soon be on your way toward authentic. Go for it!

5–8 points
Learning to Be You

You are on your way to genuine and self-contained. (In psychological speak, "self-contained" means that while you may choose to spend time with others, you don't absolutely need their company.) You probably enjoy your own company and can entertain yourself when necessary. You are moving toward real. You are getting very close. Follow the suggestions for the previous group and watch your authenticity score soar!

9–10 points
Uniquely Your Own

You are sneaking up on authenticity, and you genuinely understand and appreciate yourself. Complete and absolute authenticity is not an achievable goal. It is a goal we can pursue for an entire lifetime and never fully achieve. We are an integral part of humanity, and there is a part in each of us that is social and has a strong desire for companionship and society. Balancing the need to be who we are and yet remain connected to others is the challenge we all face.

are you for real?

If you are genuine, you are probably able to:

- perceive without judging
- live in the moment fully, without looking ahead or back
- trust your ability to guide yourself—even in a storm
- decide where you are going rather than being swept along by the tide
- use creativity to make life enjoyable and fresh

15

Are You Left-Brained or Right-Brained?

Your brain has approximately 100 billion cells, give or take one or two, forging one *quadrillion* connections. That's a lot of brainpower! Impressed?

Each brain has two "hemispheres," and our personalities are influenced by both sides. The dominant side helps determine how you view and interpret your world. Which side of your amazing brain rules your life? Are you a left-brainer: abstract concepts–loving, emotion-hiding, and organized? Or are you right-brain dominated: visual, intuitive, disorganized, meandering?

“Try to learn something about everything and everything about something.”
—*T. H. Huxley*

If you are left-brain dominated, you tend to hop right to a task, no matter how dull or uninspiring it seems. Right-brainers generally must be towed to them, kicking and screaming. Lefties (brain-lefties, that is) break down information into little chunks, line them up in an orderly fashion, and then decide what the whole thing means. Brain-righties begin with the answer and then try to understand all of the parts. If you're right-brain dominant, you may have been known to read the last pages of a mystery first, before reading the rest of the book.

Of course it's not that easy. (It never is, right?) Most people show at least some characteristics of both right and left "brainedness," and some are very nearly 50/50 on this neurological Mason-Dixon line. Naturally, their scores on this quiz will be mixed.

Are You Left-Brained or Right-Brained?

Are you a lefty or a righty?

1. When I put together a new gadget I read the directions first—every single time.

   True   *False*

2. I have been told that I'm a gifted writer, though I can't seem to spell worth a darn.

   True   *False*

3. I enjoy working with numbers.

   True   *False*

4. I have considered becoming (or am) an artist, recreation director, dancer, yoga instructor, professional athlete, marketing consultant, retail salesperson, or another occupation that allows me to be less structured and use my gift for interacting with people.

   True   *False*

5. I have considered becoming (or am) a career counselor, accountant, librarian, science teacher, computer programmer, or something else that is rule-oriented and structured.

   True   *False*

6. I have learned to listen to what my gut tells me.

   True   *False*

7. I accept changes in my life without great discomfiture—I adapt very well.

   True   *False*

8. Sure, I can adapt to change when absolutely necessary, but I prefer to change my environment to suit me—even though it sometimes causes ruffled feathers.

   True   *False*

17

Are You Left-Brained or Right-Brained?

9. Writing a paper for school or a business report is relatively easy for me.

True   *False*

10. When I give directions they sound like this: "Turn left [pointing that direction] by the church over there (you see it, right?). You will pass a yellow house with a red roof and a blue house with a rose garden in front. Continue straight for two more blocks and you'll see the ice cream store with the red-checked awning."

True   *False*

11. I try to gather all available information before I make a decision.

True   *False*

12. I try my very best to be on time, but I seldom beat the clock.

True   *False*

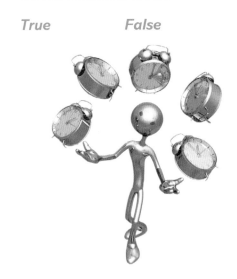

Scoring

If you answered "true" to the odd-numbered questions (or most of them), the dominant side of your brain is the left. If you answered "true" to the even questions (or most of them), you are right-brained.

Dominant Left Side

The cognitive lefties are analytical and studious and tend to be science- and math-oriented. You pay attention to the details; plan and strategize well; respond to facts, not hunches; and are practical and cautious. You probably benefit from a list to keep you on schedule and productive.

(Right-brained people also use lists, but they refuse to compromise their spontaneity.) Lefties do their best to settle in (adapt) without changing the environment. You probably respond well to strict, guided management. While right-hemisphere people tend to be good listeners, lefties are great observers. It sounds as if you have

Are You Left-Brained or Right-Brained?

Sherlock Holmes on your side. You are likely to do well on our Emotional Maturity quiz (page 28) because of your adaptability.

Dominant Right Side

You are likely to be more easily led by your emotions and are more intuitive than your left-brained counterparts. You are spontaneous and willing to follow a hunch, and you're able to see outside the box. The big picture is what interests you; you probably don't get bogged down in details. This group listens to what is being said and how it is said. This improves communication. If you fit into this group, it's likely you will do well on our Are You a Good Listener quiz (page 50). If you'd like to exercise your left brain strengths, try improving your organizational skills. That one change could make life easier for you.

Equally Right and Left

If your answers were all over the board, with no clear left or right inclination, you may be one of those unusual individuals who are more or less equally influenced by both sides of their brain. Though we all use both sides, you have more options available to you. Perhaps you have the best of both hemispheres!

the right (or left) career path

Left brain

Left-brained people generally prefer a quiet environment and enjoy fields with structured and definable job descriptions. They are logical people, talented at processing information, and tend to do well in math-related fields. Possibilities include accounting, education, medicine, any area of finance, research, and computer technology.

Right brain

If you're right-brained, think people-oriented, helping professions. Right-brained individuals usually have a need for activity and a creative environment. Good career fields include retail sales, the hospitality industry, social work, ministry, and the arts.

Which Intelligence Style Is Really You?

THERE'S MORE THAN ONE WAY TO BE SMART

In the early 1980s, Harvard professor Howard Gardner introduced the theory of multiple intelligences: simply put, the notion that different people have different styles of learning. A score from a traditional IQ test does not tell the whole story on its own—the myriad ways in which we gather and process information must also be taken into account.

Educators have labeled eight different styles of learning: Linguistic (using or writing words), Logical/Mathematical, Musical, Bodily/Kinesthetic (hands-on), Spatial/Visual, Interpersonal (in a group), Intrapersonal (alone), and Naturalist (in nature). People may use a variety of styles, but normally everyone has one dominant style that works best for them as a general rule. Everyone is unique in their own ability to learn and in the method by which they learn best. It's important to know your intelligence style if you are to compete as an employee or a student, or if you simply want to grow as a person of knowledge.

“They know enough who know how to learn.”
—*Henry Brooks Adams*

Your intelligence style is more pervasive than you might realize. It affects how you understand information, choose your words, and recall

Which Intelligence Style Is Really You?

your experiences. It's a good thing to be able to pinpoint the learning style that comes most naturally to you, because by taking advantage of your best innate intelligence skills, you will learn to shine—and you will be able to learn more with less blood, sweat, and tears.

What is your learning style?

Circle the statements that *best* apply to you.

1. When I attempt to assemble something, it just comes naturally to me.

2. I would be perfectly content keeping my accomplishments to myself.

3. I cannot talk without my hands, even when I am on the phone.

4. My career is in, or my interests lean toward, math or science.

5. I am very comfortable in nature, and I am interested in the names of trees, plants, clouds, or the like.

6. I've been told that I have a natural ability to remember names and dates.

7. I am a born leader, and I enjoy helping others reach their goals.

8. My computer needs a new router. I follow the detailed instructions rather than calling the techie hotline.

9. I prefer to study alone.

10. I love crossword puzzles.

11. At my house, the stereo is always on and I may break into a dance at any moment.

12. I visualize something in my mind to help me remember it later.

13. If I am in study-mode or learning-mode, the music is cranking.

14. I love to listen to my friends tell stories.

15. I would rather get together with my team, share some snacks, and look over the new office guidelines together than by myself.

16. I learn best when I can get outside the walls of the library, office, or lecture hall.

Which Intelligence Style Is Really You?

Learning Profiles

Linguistic

Statements **6 and 14** indicate a Linguistic intelligence style. Linguistic learners (also called "verbal" or "audible" learners) are excited by words. Given something or someone they can listen to, they are happy—and talented. Linguistic learners generally do well in lecture courses.

Logical/Mathematical

Did you circle statements **4 and 8?** If so, you have a gift for numbers and reasoning: You fall under the Logical/Mathematical category. You are comfort-able conceptualizing, and you are a logical, orderly thinker. You may enjoy brain games that require strong concentration and reasoning.

Musical

Musical learners groove to the tune of statements **11 and 13.** If your friends are looking for a rocking good time, they know where to find it. Even at your desk, the rhythm is going and you are tapping your fingers or stomping your feet.

Bodily/Kinesthetic

If you circled statements **1 and 3,** you are a Bodily/Kinesthetic learner—a hands-on type of learner. You like making things, acting out, and touching. You are prob-ably also a lover of physical activities.

Interpersonal

If you selected statements **7 and 15** your primary intelligence is Interpersonal. You are a team player—both for entertain-ment and for learning. You thrive in a group environ-ment. Your friends enjoy your attention and often come to you with their problems.

Which Intelligence Style Is Really You?

Spatial/Visual

Do statements **10 and 12** describe you? If so, you fall under the Spatial/Visual learner category. You draw pictures—figuratively and literally. Your world is a collage of images, both internal and external. You probably remember what you see quite vividly.

Intrapersonal

Statements **2 and 9** are indicators of an Intrapersonal intelligence style. Intra-personal learners know what they want out of life and are adept at reaching their goals. If you are an Intrapersonal learner, you enjoy quiet time to reflect and recharge. You may be quiet, but people listen to you when you speak.

Naturalist

If you have a Naturalist intel-ligence style you probably chose statements **5 and 16**—you are tuned in to the basic, the natural, the outdoors. You feel your best in naturalistic settings, and that is where you shine.

mixing it up

Even though people have one dominant intelligence, everyone is a mixture of all of them. No matter what your dominant style is, it would be helpful to work on improving your less-dominant styles, because sometimes we don't have the opportunity to choose our learning experiences.

If you don't enjoy reading, for example, try reading short articles or blogs on topics about which you are passionate. If you aren't a big music fan, try listening to different genres of artists, going to concerts, or learning to play an instrument. It never hurts to broaden your horizons.

What Do Your Dreams Say About You?

What do your dreams mean? Well, for some people they mean a best-selling book. Both Stephanie Meyer (*Twilight* series) and Mary Shelley *(Frankenstein)* based their popular books on a dream, or, in Shelley's case, a nightmare. Their dreams showcased their extraordinary talent. Dreams can also mean your mind is working on something and it doesn't rest while you get your Z's.

Sigmund Freud believed dreams revealed aspects of his patients' personalities. When he interpreted dreams, he was following a nebulous pathway to pathology. According to Freud, dreams reflect the suppressed urges that are frowned on in polite society. However, Freud saw suppressed urges and sex under every rock, so we must assume his fixation influenced his theory about dreams.

"Dreams are the touchstones of our character."
—*Henry David Thoreau*

While research indicates certain theories about dreams, there are also legends, cultural beliefs, and myths. What do your dreams reveal about you?

What Do Your Dreams Say About You?

Perchance to dream

1. I have very scary dreams that keep reminding me of a frightening real experience.

   True   *False*

2. I often dream I am falling, and I wake with a jerk (a muscle twitch—not a guy).

   True   *False*

3. Most of the time I don't remember my dreams.

   True   *False*

4. I dream in color.

   True   *False*

5. I have had a dream that came true.

   True   *False*

6. I have influenced a dream by concentrating on it before I fell asleep.

   True   *False*

7. I have tried to analyze my dreams.

   True   *False*

8. I believe that dreams are simply random electrical impulses without meaning.

   True   *False*

9. I occasionally dream that I am naked in a public place, humiliated and distressed.

   True   *False*

10. I believe that dreams are spiritual—a window to the unknown.

    True   *False*

What Do Your Dreams Say About You?

Summary

1. If you answered "true," you have probably had a traumatic experience and you are trying to resolve the strong emotions you feel. You are not alone; this happens to many individuals. You are striving for an answer. Good for you.

2. Some studies indicate we are born with a fear of falling. Perhaps that is why you may dream you are falling and then wake when your body jumps. This phenomenon is called *hynic jerk*, and it's relatively common. It may mean that you are sleep-deprived or reluctant to fall asleep. If you aren't getting enough sleep, you may need to work on that. If you are reluctant to go to sleep, we must wonder why. Are you having nightmares? If so, read number 6.

3. If you don't remember your dreams, it may mean you are not particularly interested in dreams. It may also mean you are not a light sleeper. You may be a well-rested, healthy, cognitive person who is not into interpreting dreams.

4. Most people dream in color. Individuals who particularly value color may be more likely to remember it from

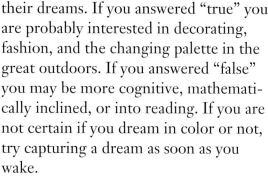

their dreams. If you answered "true" you are probably interested in decorating, fashion, and the changing palette in the great outdoors. If you answered "false" you may be more cognitive, mathematically inclined, or into reading. If you are not certain if you dream in color or not, try capturing a dream as soon as you wake.

5. Some individuals believe that dreams can predict the future. If you answered "true," you are open to many possibilities. You don't require absolute proof to consider the unusual. An open mind is very adaptive.

6. If you answered "true," you are interested in controlling your experience, even while you sleep. Yes, dreams can be controlled; therapists have used this method for years to help clients conquer recurrent nightmares. Try this yourself: Think about what you want to dream for a few minutes before you go to sleep each night. This takes practice; don't give up.

What Do Your Dreams Say About You?

7. If you have attempted to analyze your dream, you are curious and open to possibilities. You want to learn more about yourself (which is also why you are reading a personality quiz book!). One's interpretation of a dream is often linked to what he or she was concerned about at that time.

If you have not analyzed your dreams, you are more interested in facts than in the world of dreams. A rational, logical focus has probably worked quite well for you, and you are comfortable with factual data. Your left brain is most likely your dominant hemisphere. (See our Left Brain/Right Brain quiz on page 16.)

8. If you said "true," you fit the rational, logical mold from number 7. The theory of random electrical impulses makes good, logical sense. However, it is only a theory—and not the most popular theory.

If you did not gravitate toward the electrical impulses theory, you are keeping your imagination open and hoping for a more interesting explanation.

9. There is a common belief that clothes are a metaphor for our public, "masked" selves and that being naked in public signifies showing all of our secrets to the world. Or, it may mean there is an embarrassing situation in your life and the dream is a symbolic way of exploring the issue. Until the real life issue is resolved, the dream may continue to occur. Conversely, if you have the bare-bottom dream and do not feel humiliated or embarrassed, this may be a sign that you are seeking freedom from convention.

10. If you believe your dreams are spiritual in nature, you have a very strong spiritual consciousness. There are legends, myths, and religious teachings that are congruent with your belief. Iroquois Native American lore suggests that dreams are a guide to help people make wise choices and decisions. Many other cultures have had similar beliefs.

lucid dreaming

Lucid dreaming means you are aware that you are dreaming. If you notice you are doing or seeing something that is impossible, such as flying without wings, your dream self realizes that you must be dreaming. Perhaps you are more imaginative than the average person and you enjoy the wonderful land where anything can happen—and often does.

Are You Emotionally Mature?

Relationships and careers are built on a foundation of emotional maturity. No matter how attractive, witty, or intelligent we might be, these characteristics mean virtually nothing unless we have learned to control our emotional responses to life. True, most people are drawn to cool and humorous individuals, but be assured, these superficial attractions wear thin very quickly if there is no emotional maturity for support.

Emotional maturity means understanding your strengths and your weaknesses and using them to your best advantage. The ability to connect with others in

"Maturity begins to grow when you can sense your concern for others beginning to outweigh your concern for yourself."
—*John MacNaughton*

a cooperative manner is a sign of emotional maturity. Our emotions make life interesting and exciting. Without our virtually unlimited variety of feelings we would be little more than soft, well-dressed robots. Nonetheless, emotions have the potential to become California wildfires, burning out of control and destroying everything in their path.

Are You Emotionally Mature?

Are you a firecracker or the Rock of Gibraltar?

How well do these statements match your emotional IQ? Put a checkmark in the appropriate box.

	Agree	It's a toss-up	Disagree
1. Friendships are valuable; I find time to smooth spats.	☐	☐	☐
2. Jealousy is a wasteful emotion; I avoid it.	☐	☐	☐
3. Being rejected isn't fun, but I handle it and go on.	☐	☐	☐
4. I am loved, and I give love.	☐	☐	☐
5. I am not perfect, but I am a good person.	☐	☐	☐
6. I am solution-oriented—I don't occupy myself with worries.	☐	☐	☐
7. I have no control over others—and I really don't want control.	☐	☐	☐
8. Yes, I can handle issues on my own, though I like talking with my friends as a reality test.	☐	☐	☐

Are You Emotionally Mature?

	Agree	It's a toss-up	Disagree
9. I am adaptive when things change— I can modify my behaviors without undue stress.	☐	☐	☐
10. I am relatively stress-free.	☐	☐	☐
11. I enjoy giving, though I am also appreciative of receiving.	☐	☐	☐
12. Most of the time I do a good job.	☐	☐	☐
13. I normally understand my emotions and what caused them.	☐	☐	☐
14. I know that people will criticize me sometimes—I can live with that.	☐	☐	☐
15. My friends and I talk about our emotions and thoughts.	☐	☐	☐
16. My friends say I am always the same, and they know what to expect from me. They like that.	☐	☐	☐
17. I can convert anger into productive energy.	☐	☐	☐
18. My friends have said that I am easy to get along with.	☐	☐	☐

Are You Emotionally Mature?

Scoring

Give yourself **1 point** for "Disagree," **2 points** for "It's a toss-up," and **3 points** for "Agree." Tally your points and look for your profile below.

18–24 points
You're Growing

Perhaps you feel some discomfort and would like to make a few positive changes in your life. Emotional excess or relationship issues due to emotional upheaval can create a great deal of distress. You may want to ask yourself where your limitations lie. Once you understand what you need to make your life more satisfying, you can start in that direction. Perhaps discussing these issues with a trusted friend would help.

25–39 points
You're Getting There

You are generally quite happy with your life and relationships, but there may be times when you struggle emotionally. Your friends appreciate your genuine warmth; however, sometimes they may be concerned about your emotional intensity. If that's the case, possibly you want to level out the hills and valleys and become more laid-back. Intensity can be exciting and energizing, although most of us would agree that a little intensity goes a long way. If your emotions are not in balance, you may be feeling some subtle symptoms of stress, such as an occasional headache, upset stomach, or muscle tension. If so, exercise and relaxation could help reduce your stress level.

40–54 points
You're There

You have long-lasting, strong relationships, and you feel good about yourself and your life. You can be trusted not to go off like a Roman candle or to weep into your beer. (Sure, we all have bad days. Cut yourself some slack for the occasional "off" day.)

Do You Have an Awesome Sense of Humor?

When we laugh we feel happy, more self-confident, and more connected to others, and the truth is, we probably are all of those things at that moment.

How does a full-throated, tummy-tickling laugh make you feel? It feels great, doesn't it? Writer Charles Dickens thought it felt wonderful: He once said he wanted only to be introduced to someone with a gut-clutching laugh, and he would make that person a friend for life. Simply put, we love to laugh, and we value the people who bring laughter to our lives.

"The most wasted day of all is that on which we have not laughed."
—*Nicolas Chamfort*

Did you know that laughter actually makes people healthier? A real belly laugh relieves stress, burns calories, gives your midsection a good workout, and even aids in digestion. Studies indicate that a sense of humor and a jolly laugh can even help protect against heart disease. Who knew that whomever said "laughter is the best medicine" actually meant it?

What else is laughter good for? Well, besides good health and good times, it may also be your ticket to a world-class love life. When asked what they found attractive in a partner, both men and women listed "sense of humor" in the top five on their list of "must have" characteristics. In other words: Make me laugh, and I'm yours.

Do You Have an Awesome Sense of Humor?

How ticklish is your funny bone?

1. I know how to giggle at myself, laugh with others, and enjoy the irony of life.

   True   *False*

2. "Indubitably" and "certainly" sound the same to me.

   True   *False*

3. My friends tell me I am quirky (or funny). I hope that means humorous.

   True   *False*

4. It's difficult for me to find irony in the most serious situations.

   True   *False*

5. My friends' jokes are generally not very funny, especially the ones I have heard before.

   True   *False*

6. Given my choice of movie on a hot date, I'd go for the drama or thriller over the comedy.

   True   *False*

7. I forward the hilarious e-mails I receive to all my friends. (I delete the lame ones. If they don't make me laugh they're not worth my time.)

   True   *False*

8. I believe that life is outrageous, and I cannot wait for the next chapter.

   True   *False*

9. I will love you if you tell me a good joke. I will absolutely adore you if, over and over again, you tickle my funny bone.

   True   *False*

10. I've been known to sit at my computer and chuckle to myself until my coworkers think it's time they sent me on a vacation.

    True   *False*

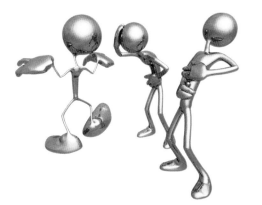

Do You Have an Awesome Sense of Humor?

Answers

1. True. Why stop at one source of wittiness? Laugh at them all.

2. False. One theory of comedy suggests that some words and numbers are inherently funny. Frequently, the funny words say something in a bizarre or odd way. The sound of the word also plays a role in the chuckle factor.

3. True. Your friends notice and appreciate your marvelous sense of the totally ridiculous.

4. False. As poet/novelist Leonard Cohen said: "There is a crack in everything. That's how the light gets in."

5. False. Laughter makes your friends feel good and increases your wellness, so laugh at every opportunity.

6. False. What better way to spend an evening than laughing with someone?

7. True. Gotta spread the wealth—a joke might brighten someone's day.

8. True. Optimism is a form of good humor.

9. True. How to attract friends and lovers: Entertain them.

10. True. What's so funny: your coworkers, your boss, an e-mail from a friend? It doesn't matter, as long as the laughter lightens your workload for a while.

humor has it

Charmers may be narcissists, beauties might be airheads, and brilliance is sometimes soooo boring, but a good sense of humor never grows old—it deepens and sharpens with age. An easy choice, no?

Do You Have an Awesome Sense of Humor?

Scoring

Add up your points, and find your profile below. Give yourself **1 point** for each matching answer. (Give yourself an extra point or two if you laughed while taking this quiz.)

0–3 points
The Smiler

Come on, surely there's something you find funny. So maybe you don't think "Who's on First" is a classic or set your DVR to record *Saturday Night Live* every week, but perhaps you've found yourself smiling at a coworker's joke or have been amused by the antics of your three-year-old niece. Go back to this quiz and give yourself some more points; you'll be happier.

4–7 points
The Chuckler

You have a well-developed sense of the preposterous. At times, you can laugh at yourself and the rest of the world. Your friends and family enjoy your silly/fun side. You may like to hang out with a crowd who also enjoys laughing.

8–10+ points
The Belly-laugher

Jerry Seinfeld...Jon Stewart...Chris Rock...Rita Rudner...Robin Williams...YOU! As Mr. Williams once said, "You're only given a little spark of madness. You mustn't lose it." You've got that spark, and then some. You're lucky enough to find humor in the mundane, and generous enough to share your laughter with others. Keep enjoying life—there's plenty to laugh at every day, and when there's not, you know how to create it on your own.

what is "funny"?

Everybody has their own unique sense of humor. Some people are silly, some are dry and sophisticated, some can't help but guffaw at locker-room jokes.

Defining the essence of funny is impossible. What's funny to you might make someone else shake their head in bewilderment; what's a laugh riot to them might offend your sensibilities. This quiz simply identifies a few of the familiar symptoms. As E. B. White said, "Analyzing humor is like dissecting a frog. Few people are interested, and the frog dies of it."

Are You Intuitive?

If someone says you are intuitive, they are referring to how you take in information from the outside world. This is revealed through your thoughts, beliefs,

> **"The intuitive mind is a sacred gift and the rational mind is a faithful servant."**
> —*Albert Einstein*

and behaviors. Intuitive types tend to be relatively optimistic, "big-picture" oriented, and innovative. It's quite common for intuitive types to be misunderstood and—sometimes—scorned by more concrete, "show-me" types of people. Intuitive people often dance to the beat of a different drummer, and others may not recognize their valuable contributions. This lack of understanding may cause them to doubt their ability and reasoning skills.

Intuitive individuals are usually quite bright, with an innate ability to grasp complex data and quickly understand it. Albert Einstein, Sigmund Freud, Hillary Clinton, Donald Trump, and the fictional Sherlock Holmes probably are (or were) highly intuitive. Though they are very different individuals, they share the ability to see what could be—as well as what is.

Are you innately enabled?

Which response most closely matches your personality?

	Not even close	It's hard to say	Right on
1. I remember the past and focus on the future, but sometimes I miss the little nagging trifles here in the present (such as organizing my desk or scheduling my time).	☐	☐	☐

Are You Intuitive?

	Not even close	It's hard to say	Right on
2. My fear, if I have one, is about what will happen to me next month or next year.	☐	☐	☐
3. I take great delight in the novel, the quaint, and the new.	☐	☐	☐
4. My friends or teachers have called me a daydreamer.	☐	☐	☐
5. I am adept at viewing large chunks of information and understanding it with a few quick scans.	☐	☐	☐
6. I spend a lot of time searching for lost keys, glasses, passwords, or books.	☐	☐	☐
7. I am likely to accept blame when relationships and communication break down.	☐	☐	☐
8. I have been applauded for my creativity and innovative flair.	☐	☐	☐
9. Though I have many novel and imaginative ideas, I find follow-through a lackluster endeavor.	☐	☐	☐
10. I shudder to think how much time my more organized friends put into useless, repetitive chores.	☐	☐	☐

Are You Intuitive?

Scoring

Give yourself **1 point** for every "Not even close," **2 points** for every "It's hard to say," and **3 points** for each "Right on."

10–15 points
Seeing the Trees

You are probably more sensing than intuitive, which means you are more concrete and earthbound. You are comfortable with facts and figures and the here and now. You are probably exceptionally efficient at detail-oriented tasks, and you may get frustrated by the intuitive folks—though, incidentally, studies indicate that it is quite likely you will chose one as your life companion.

16–24 points
Seeing the Forest and the Trees

You could lean in either direction from your perch on top of the fence. You are likely to get along with the imaginative *and* the concrete. You may very well be equally right-brained and left-brained (take the quiz on page 16 to find out). You would probably function well in a structured career, yet be creative when the task calls for it. You may learn from the past, live in the present, and prepare for the future.

24–30 points
Seeing the Forest

No matter what you may have heard to the contrary, your brain functions quite well. You may have struggled in high school, yet your academic performance probably improved significantly in college. That's because high school is often designed for the ordered student—not for imaginative, spontaneous, "out of the box" teens.

You have probably found your niche in a career that values your notable talents. Many talented writers, professors, actors, and artists are intuitive. That should give your self-esteem a well-deserved boost.

CHAPTER 2

YOUR RELATIONSHIPS

Nothing brings us more happiness than our healthy relationships with friends, family, and coworkers. Relationship skills are essential to our enjoyment of life and to our wellness.

Friends are a joy and a delight. Learn your friendship score and how to be the best friend you can be. Do you give enough to the people you care about? Discover whether you are a giver or a taker, and learn how to be a world-class listener.

Not everyone is as truthful as they think they are. Find out if the truth police are after you. Would you like to be granted the gift to see yourself as others see you? If so, it's time to determine if your self-image is accurate. Learn about body language to see if you need an interpreter.

The quizzes in this chapter will let you know how well you relate to the people in your life.

Are You a Tried and True Friend?

How would your friends rate you as a friend? Are you a "pass-me-the-tissue" and "you-go-girl" true-blue friend?

How would you rate your friends? Are they the awesome real deal, or are they the fair-weather variety: there for you as long as it's convenient for them?

Friends don't have to be perfect. They just need to be there when you need them. When we are with our loyal friends, we feel comfortable and welcome. They are always delighted to see us. When you walk into the room, a friend's face will glow with a

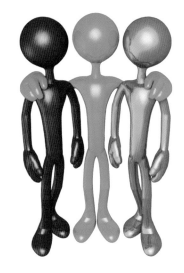

"Friend. Good."
—*Frankenstein's monster*

welcoming smile—you can feel the warmth all the way to your toes. Now, that's what friends are. Whether you need a bud to help you celebrate, a shoulder for weeping, or just an evening of movies and popcorn, this is the kind of friend you want—and so do your friends.

being a good friend

We're not always at our best, and friends know that and are willing to cut us some slack. However, moodiness or cold behavior should be the exception rather than the rule in friendship. It's allowable in small doses, but don't overdo it.

Are You a Tried and True Friend?

Are you true-blue?

Pick the response that is most in tune with your friendship philosophy. There will be more than one right answer, but there is only one best answer.

1. You and your main squeeze are planning a romantic weekend getaway. Just as you're packing your bag, your friend Melly sends a text telling you her love relationship has just exploded. What do you do?

    a. I know it's terrible, but I'm in a hurry. I won't answer right now.

    b. I text back right away, telling her that my heart is with her, but if I don't take this trip my romance may blow up as well.

    c. I invite her to join us on the trip. After all, friends come first.

    d. I tell her I'll be right over—just give me a moment to break the news to my sweetie.

2. You and your best bud Tiff pool your money to buy a few lotto tickets. To your utter amazement, one of the tickets wins a very cool $100,000. What do you do?

    a. Wow, this is so totally fabulous! I can't wait to call Tiff.

    b. Well, it *was* my idea. She hasn't said another word about it. And she only put in 10 bucks to my 20.

    c. Hmmmm, I need to give this some thought. I'll call Tiff tomorrow.

    d. Good for Tiff! She could use a vacation on a warm beach, wearing a hot bikini and enjoying a cool beverage.

3. Thanksgiving is fast approaching, and it's time to make your plans. Your family is far away, and you've been invited to sup with three different friends. What do you do?

    a. I cook a fabulous dinner at my house and invite all my friends.

    b. I invite my friends to get together for a potluck.

    c. I hide behind the couch with my favorite novel until Thanksgiving passes.

    d. I find out which local restaurants are serving Thanksgiving dinner.

Are You a Tried and True Friend?

4. It's your best friend's birthday, and you're in the middle of a serious economic downturn. Your friend gave you a fancy new iPod for your birthday. Now what will you do?

    a. I rummage through the "re-gift" closet for a likely prospect.

    b. I offer to spend my next day off detailing her new car.

    c. I "forget" her birthday and hide out, mortified that I don't have the wherewithal for an expensive gift.

    d. I promise to buy an awesome gift for her when my ship comes in.

5. What is your friendship motto?

    a. Friends 'til the end (but the end comes when you look at my guy).

    b. You need me, buddy? I'm there!

    c. Friends come first—unless I'm seriously busy.

    d. We are the dearest of pals—unless you insinuate that I am not perfect or you show your flaws.

6. Your friend (who tends to be a bit critical) asks you if he or she is too critical. How do you respond?

    a. Well, I, ah, you know, I—wow, is it really that late? I've gotta run!

    b. Critical? What exactly do you mean by the word critical?

    c. Lots of people are more critical than you are.

    d. Why do you ask? Let's sit down and talk about it.

7. You and your lover are having some personal problems. How much do you share with your friends?

    a. I spill it all—every tiny detail.

    b. I want someone to tell me I'm right! I share every single one of my lover's faults and minimize my own tiny flaws.

    c. I ask for support from my friends without demonizing my lover.

    d. I keep the pain to myself; I'm the one who counsels everyone else.

Are You a Tried and True Friend?

8. Your friend and coworker, George, tells you he plans to leave his job and go to work for the competition—with a promotion and a great raise! He asks you to keep his plans under wraps. Do you?

   a. George is a friend. I keep my promise to respect his secret.

   b. I tell the boss. Showing a little loyalty to the company can't hurt my prospects.

   c. I don't break my promise to George, but I drop a few hints—if they figure it out on their own, it's not my fault.

   d. I pretend I didn't hear him and suddenly get busy with my e-mail.

9. Your friend Priscilla calls you and shrills, "I just traded in my old Honda for a brand-new Chrysler Prowler!" Hmm, Priscilla is generally the most levelheaded and frugal person imaginable. What do you do?

   a. I run to my computer and start googling therapists in our area.

   b. I ask her to take me for a ride; I could use a little excitement too.

   c. I talk with her to find out what prompted this wildly uncharacteristic decision. Then I decide what to do.

   d. She's a grown woman; this is none of my business.

Answers

Give yourself **1 point** for each "best" answer you chose.

1. (d) When the worst happens, friends are there for us—totally there for us.

2. (d) Good friends want the very best for each other. "A" is not a bad answer, either.

3. (b) Yes, we want to pamper our friends, but there is something to be said for the reciprocity principle. Let your friends do their share and contribute their yummy recipes. It will be a magnificent Thanksgiving, and it won't stress anyone out.

4. (b) You have something special that you can give right now. Her car will look glorious, and she'll appreciate your hard work. When you go the extra mile to show your love, it shines.

Are You a Tried and True Friend?

5. (b) A friend we can depend on no matter what is the friend we all want.

6. (d) Friends support us and stand beside us, right or wrong. However, sometimes the best thing you can do for a friend is to help him or her to grow. Sit down and talk about it.

7. (c) If you tell all and make your lover look like a jerk, what are you going to say if you make up? Your friends may remain outraged long after you and your sweetie have kissed and made up.

8. (a) Unless someone will be harmed, we keep our friends' confidences. No if, ands, or buts…end of story.

9. (c) She may have had an extreme "stress" episode, though it is unlikely. Take a few minutes to discuss her reasoning process when she made her decision. If she can tell you the current year, who the president is, and how she plans to pay for the car, she's probably okay. Enjoy an exciting new experience—hit the road together.

Scoring

Give yourself **1 point** for each matching answer.

0–4 points
A Friend in Training
You are not always a tried and true friend. Perhaps you really want to be a fabulous friend, the person we all want to hang with. We attract people who are similar to ourselves. You need and deserve loyal, considerate, and rock-solid friends. To obtain these relationships, begin by being the friend you want to have. Question your friendship philosophy, and give it a few nips and tucks.

5–9 points
A Friend Indeed
You are a moderate to fabulous friend. You are the bud we call when we need a shoulder to cry on or someone to help celebrate our triumphs. You understand balance, which is as important in friendship as it is in every other aspect of life. You didn't need a quiz to prove that you are an exceptional friend; your large number of friends and the depth of those friendships is all the evidence you'll ever need.

Are You a Giver or a Taker?

As you may have noticed, the world is populated with both thoughtful givers and entitled takers. These two personality types seem to gravitate toward each other with an unfailing sense of direction that's superior even to the most high-tech GPS system. Though you may not spend a large chunk of your time thinking about whom among your friends, or which of the celebrities that flit across your screen, belongs to which group—let's face it, you know. Where would you pencil in Paris Hilton? How about Mother Teresa? Okay, those two are entirely too obvious. What if we raise the complexity bar? There's a third group: individuals who have settled into a balanced blend of giver/taker.

> **We exist temporarily through what we take, but we live forever through what we give.**
> —*Douglas M. Lawson*

It's pretty obvious that takers are not the best relationship choice. Yet there must be some advantages to freely accumulating goods and services, or there would be fewer takers. Are takers altogether bad? On the flip side, can givers overdo a good thing? Hmmm, one of humankind's everlasting, perhaps unanswerable, questions.

Are You a Giver or a Taker?

Are you a saint or a sinner?

For each question, choose the response that more closely matches your thoughts.

1. It's the last day of work before the holidays, and the gang is heading out to down some cranberry martinis and holiday treats. It's been a long week; I can't wait to join them. But a coworker just presented me with a last-minute, unexpected gift. I don't have anything for him.

   a. I run out into the vast, daunting throng of manic shoppers to buy a thoughtful gift in return.

   b. I clap him on the back and thank him earnestly for his thoughtfulness.

2. I am standing in a long line at my neighborhood megastore, and a frazzled-looking mother with a pair of chocolate-smeared munchkins in tow pushes ahead of me in line.

   a. I grit my teeth, tense my jaw muscles, smile, and don't say anything.

   b. I politely but firmly inform her she just cut in front of me, and ask her to please wait her turn.

3. I normally arrive at work with the birds and leave with the cleaning crew. It is Friday night and I have plans for some fun, for a change—and my boss asks me to stay late to finish a project my coworker bungled.

   a. I roll up my sleeves and settle in to help.

   b. I shut down my computer, look my boss in the eye, and say, "Shoot, I can't. Important plans— gotta run."

❝The hand that gives, gathers.❞
—James Howell

Are You a Giver or a Taker?

4. I am totally content, caught up in a gripping page-turner and luxuriating in the warmth of my cozy hearth, when suddenly my Norman Rockwell moment is shattered by the ring of the telephone. A friend pleads with me to pick her up downtown after a particularly fun happy hour.

   a. I sigh, put down my book, and grab the car keys.

   b. I let her know I'm in the middle of something and offer to call her a cab.

5. I spend hours choosing the perfect birthday gifts for my friends. They don't seem to put much thought into picking up a gift for me—when they do buy a gift.

   a. That's okay; their friendship is all I want or need.

   b. Would it kill them to return the favor? That's it— no gifts for them next year.

6. The object of my affection has been especially inattentive: not returning my phone calls, forgetting our plans, or canceling at the last minute. Of course, I understand: He's in a bad mood, he had a bad day, work was particularly strenuous, his boss has it out for him. . . .

   a. He simply needs an affirming, sympathetic ear and unconditional positive regard—from me.

   b. Uh-uh. Regardless of what's going on at work, he'd better start treating me right or I'm going to hit the road.

7. I work at staying connected to my friends. I e-mail, call, text, send e-cards, and generally assure friends that they are important to me. I don't always hear back right away.

   a. That's okay—I know how busy they are, and I don't mind making the extra effort.

   b. How rude. What am I—chopped liver?

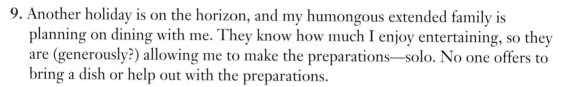

Are You a Giver or a Taker?

8. I am a volunteer extraordinaire. I staff hotlines and heap plates with food at the local soup kitchen. I sell candy (and popcorn, magazines, cookie dough—you name it) to raise money for schools. I walk my neighbor's dogs. I pick up litter in my neighborhood.

    a. This is so rewarding. I'm glad I can do my part to help.

    b. I wonder if everyone knows how much time and effort I put into this?

9. Another holiday is on the horizon, and my humongous extended family is planning on dining with me. They know how much I enjoy entertaining, so they are (generously?) allowing me to make the preparations—solo. No one offers to bring a dish or help out with the preparations.

    a. I start my shopping list and begin polishing the silver.

    b. I start a phone chain going, assigning everyone a specific dish to bring.

10. I am getting ready for a spectacular night of club hopping—it seems like forever since I've had a night out on the town! I search desperately for my slinky new dress (two weeks salary), but I can't find it anywhere. I hear a knock on my door, and my roommate walks in wearing the missing dress (ooh, it is as great as I remember).

    a. Okay, I'll find something else to wear. Shoot, I really do look great in that dress.

    b. I march her right back to her room and give her three minutes to hand over the dress.

Are You a Giver or a Taker?

Scoring

Give yourself **1 point** for each "a" answer.

0–3 points
What's Mine Is Mine

You are unambiguous and totally consistent. You'll never be confused with a door-mat—and it's a safe bet to say sainthood is out of the question. People certainly do

Just say no

not take advantage of you or expect you to be overly indulgent. You're perfectly comfortable saying no; in fact, you may say, "What part of no do you not understand?" It's not a sin to say no, and you know this. But sometimes you do say yes—and then you're on the side of the angels.

4–7 points
What's Ours Is Ours

You are generous, yet you expect to receive something in return for your efforts. There's nothing wrong with that! You don't mind saying no to unreasonable requests, but you believe in reciprocity, too: Fair is fair. Enjoy your relationships; they are strong, balanced, and satisfying. Although sainthood is unlikely, don't despair. As Billy Joel sang, "I'd rather laugh with the sinners than cry with the saints; the sinners are much more fun."

8–10 points
What's Mine Is Yours

You are exceptionally generous and giving. You have given without expecting (or getting) much in return. Your friends understand the limits of your generosity: There are none! You give until it hurts

and then give a tad more. Generosity is wonderful; just make sure you don't feel taken advantage of. Remember, it's okay to say no occasionally: No one will hold it against you!

The criteria for sainthood are right-eousness and being dead, and in order to be named a saint one must have per-formed miracles while living. You are well on your way. Congratulations!

Are You a Good Listener?

The ability to hear is standard; the ability to *listen* is a choice. When we listen and show that we are listening, we give the gift of undivided attention. Think about it. Do you remember the last time someone actually paid close attention to what you said, looked at you, nodded now and again, and did not interrupt you with questions or comments? Being heard is a great compliment; it means we are important enough to be given a valuable gift— full attention. If you want to be popular, appreciated, and hailed as an exceptional human being, try listening and *showing* that you are listening.

For some mysterious reason, many people underutilize their hearing apparatus. Perhaps we enjoy talking about ourselves and our interests more than hearing about something we may not find interesting. Also, we are bombarded by thousands of bits of stimuli every day: television, iPods, e-mail, cell phones, text messaging—communication overload!

> **❝I know that you believe you understand what you think I said, but I'm not sure you realize that what you heard is not what I meant.❞**
>
> —*Robert McCloskey*

Nonetheless, research suggests that communication is at the heart of intimate relationships. If we want to succeed in our careers and maintain close personal relationships, effective listening skills are vital. Not listening could be interpreted as not caring— not good.

Are You a Good Listener?

Listen up!

. . . .

1. Sure, I'm busy, but I find the time to listen to troubled friends and family.

True   *False*

2. I have many friends who phone, text-message, e-mail, and visit me.

True   *False*

3. I am so tuned in to people I can finish their sentences—even folks I barely know.

True   *False*

4. My friends are so strange—they often swear they've told me things that I'm sure they never said.

True   *False*

5. Don't you just hate people who can't get to the point? I mean they just go on and on and they never say anything that means anything. You know what I am saying? Just on and on, man. I mean, come on, what's their point?

True   *False*

6. I did well in lecture classes in school.

True   *False*

7. When I am concentrating on what someone is saying, I lean forward and make eye contact.

True   *False*

8. When we are planning an evening out, my sweetie reminds me numerous times where and when we are meeting. True, I tend to be late, and I've even been known to go to the wrong place, but not every time.

True   *False*

9. Just to be certain I understand what someone is telling me, I will paraphrase what he or she is saying and repeat it back to them.

True   *False*

10. I check my e-mail while talking on the phone, because I find that I save hours each day by multitasking.

True   *False*

Are You a Good Listener?

Answers

Give yourself **1 point** for each matching answer.

1. True. You manage to find time to stay connected to your friends. This "person-centered" philosophy works very well for you.

2. True. You are obviously doing something right. You wouldn't have so many devoted friends if you weren't a world-class listener.

3. False. Every once in a while it is okay to finish someone's sentence—when you know them really, really well. Otherwise, it simply annoys people.

4. False. Either they really are strange, or, more likely, you are not listening to their messages.

5. False. I don't think this needs an explanation, man, you know what I'm saying?

6. True. Many people are linguistic (verbal) learners (they learn by listening to someone else speak)*; thus they tend to be good listeners.

7. True. Listening comes naturally to you, and people can see that. They are probably quite likely to want to talk to you.

8. False. Not picking up on important information is a sign of distracted attention. You have probably noticed that friends will continue to repeat their messages until you catch on. Or else... they'll find someone who *will* listen to them.

9. True. Absolutely, if you are unsure what someone means, repeat away. You want to make sure you don't miss anything.

10. False. You are a fabulous multitasker; unfortunately, this is a quiz on listening, not multitasking. Performing two tasks simultaneously reduces your optimal performance for both tasks.

For more on auditory learning, see our Intelligence Style quiz on page 20.

Are You a Good Listener?

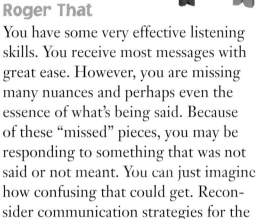

Scoring

0–3 points
Hello? Is Anybody Out There?
A communication wizard you are not. You may excel at speaking—even public speaking—however, you are missing essential chunks of conversation. Perhaps you could pick up a few cues from some of your friends who are champion listeners. Watch and learn, or—better—*listen* and learn.

You may be tightly wound and find it difficult to stay in one place long enough to listen; if so, take deep breaths to slow your nervous system down. Or maybe you're a highly respected, cognitive "professor" sort, living quite happily within your cognitive domain. You may not even hear what others are say-

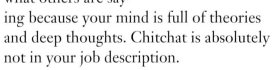

ing because your mind is full of theories and deep thoughts. Chitchat is absolutely not in your job description.

4–7 points
Roger That
You have some very effective listening skills. You receive most messages with great ease. However, you are missing many nuances and perhaps even the essence of what's being said. Because of these "missed" pieces, you may be responding to something that was not said or not meant. You can just imagine how confusing that could get. Reconsider communication strategies for the questions on which you got 0 points, and practice good listening. You can do it!

8–10 points
Coming Through Loud and Clear
You are paying attention to what others are saying, and listening with great interest. Because you are getting the entire message, you are able to respond appropriately. Whether you realize it or not, you are following the good listener rule of 80/20: In conversations we should listen 80 percent of the time and talk 20 percent of the time.

Are You Truthful?

Do you think you're a truthful person? You may be like George Washington (you cannot tell a lie)—but there's a chance that you're a little less truthful than you think. There's more than one kind of lying, and not all of them are necessarily bad. There's bending, stretching, circumnavigating, or embroidering the truth . . . and then there's fabricating, mutilating, or otherwise rendering it unrecognizable.

> **"Whoever is careless with the truth in small matters cannot be trusted with important matters."**
>
> —Albert Einstein

Sometimes people don't mean to lie, but they settle for a little white one rather than risk hurting someone's feelings. A white lie can be nicer ("No, that dress doesn't make you look heavy"), quicker ("No, no, I haven't been waiting long at all"), or just plain easier to tell than the whole truth. Explaining exactly why you don't have your homework can be complicated and not especially convincing. Sometimes it's just easier to say, "I forgot."

Is lying really lying if the person doesn't know that he or she is being a bit loose with the truth? Remember, the "truth" is frequently open for interpretation. Sometimes it's an open-and-shut case: Did you, or did you not, steal the cookie from the cookie jar? In other cases, one must question how diligently the fabricator struggled to tell the truth—and for what reasons they bent it.

Are you a kindly prevaricator; a vague, noncommittal fabricator; or the truth police?

Are You Truthful?

Do you swear to tell the truth, the whole truth, and nothing but the truth?

Choose a, b, or c (and remember—be honest!).

1. A friend asks you to critique his new manuscript. You absolutely hate it. You tell him:

  a. I love it! I think you have a best seller! *(It's awful!)*

  b. I'm not a professional editor—so I may be way off base—but I like it, although I do see some problems.

  c. I am simply amazed.

2. You have been asked to join a new social club, but you think it sounds boring. You respond:

  a. I am already scheduled for something else on those nights. Thanks, though! *(Thanks, but no thanks!)*

  b. Thanks, but that really isn't something I think I would enjoy.

  c. There are some things you just can't get around to. Right?

3. Your boss asks if you would mind staying late at work to finish a project. You tell her:

  a. No, I don't mind at all. *(Yes, I do mind!)*

  b. I promised I would be home by 8:00, so I'll see how much I can get done by then.

  c. Good workers sure have a strong work ethic, don't they?

4. Your best friend cooks a birthday dinner for you. The meal is a disaster. You say:

  a. You're a wonderful cook! This is the best meal I've ever had. *(Blech!)*

  b. This isn't what I had in mind for my birthday. Let's go to the Mexican café around the corner instead—my treat.

  c. Really, I don't believe I have ever eaten anything like this before.

5. Your main squeeze gives you a horrible brown and black sweater. You exclaim:

  a. Sweetie, I love it. It will look great with my new pants. *(U-G-L-Y!)*

  b. Unfortunately, this just isn't something I'll wear. Do you mind if I return it?

  c. You chose this all by yourself?

Are You Truthful?

6. You dent your car in a minor fender-bender. When your significant other asks about the dent you say:

   a. Fender? I don't know anything about a dented fender. *(Shoot—I'm busted!)*

   b. Yes, unfortunately, I was in an accident.

   c. So there's a dent, huh?

7. You've decided it's time to end your long-term relationship. You tell your soon-to-be ex:

   a. We have to break up; I took a job in another state. *(Please don't call me.)*

   b. I'm sorry, but I don't love you anymore. I think we should talk about going in a new direction with our relationship.

   c. Nothing. You just stop calling and hope he or she won't notice.

8. When filling out your profile for an online dating service, you are asked to include a picture of yourself. You would:

   a. Post a picture of your gorgeous cousin. *(There's a family resemblance.)*

   b. Post your most recent picture.

   c. Leave the photo area empty, and when someone asks why you didn't post a picture, respond, "What?! My picture isn't there?"

9. Are there circumstances in which it is both moral and responsible to tell an untruth?

   a. Absolutely. In fact, it happens frequently. *(Of course!)*

   b. Perhaps, but very, very rarely.

   c. You know, there are times when you just don't know what to do. Am I right?

10. When you filled out your employment application, what did you omit?

   a. I didn't omit anything—but I did slant a couple of things a tad in my favor.

   b. I didn't omit anything.

   c. HR people don't expect you to answer every question.

Are You Truthful?

Scoring

More "a" answers
Kindly Prevaricator

You are too nice to hurt anyone's feelings with an unkind truth. You make up something that will circumvent unpleasantness; in fact, you may be quite creative at serving a more palatable truth. You try to avoid confrontations and prefer playing well with others. You interpret "facts" as if they were endlessly fluid.

While avoiding unpleasantness is a worthwhile, humanitarian goal, it can cause problems with people who don't agree with your fluidity theory. You might enjoy your relationships more if you stick closer to the truth—even when it's unpleasant. If people who don't understand the value of creativity catch you in a fib, your credibility could take a hit.

More "b" answers
Truth Police

You are not interested in "deciding" if the truth is appropriate—you tell the facts without reservation. There may be a few times when tact wins over veracity, but not often. In fact, your significant other and your friends may complain about your blunt answers to questions that could be answered with, "You look fabulous, dear." When your friends want honesty, they come to you. When they want a little ego stroke or the comfort of a few kind words, however empty, they head elsewhere. But everyone needs a plain-speaking, no-nonsense friend in his or her corner—someone who will tell the hard truth, such as, "He's just not that into you." You're trustworthy, reliable, and honest, and that's the truth.

More "c" answers
Noncommittal Fabricator

You travel around the truth, quite often flirting with duplicity and deception. You may find it difficult to take a definite stand, especially if the stand might be unpopular. By responding with an ambiguous answer, you are leaving all of your options open. Unfortunately, your friends and coworkers may consider you wishy-washy, without strong values or beliefs. You may discover that you gain respect by voicing your true opinions and then letting the cards fall where they may. It will take a little practice, but you will bask in the new attention you get—a real boost to your self-esteem.

Do You See Yourself as Others See You?

Humans are expert at avoiding painful truths. Therefore, we may choose not to know how others really perceive us. If you are humble, you might

> **"O wad some Power the giftie give us To see ourselves as others see us!"**
> —Robert Burnes

be in for a delightful surprise if you start asking your friends for their opinions. If you are narcissistic, well, you may get a nasty jolt if you ask too many probing questions. Most of us fall somewhere in between, with a relatively realistic self-image.

Researchers found years ago that some characteristics are more important than others in determining how our friends and coworkers perceive us. Two of the most notable defining characteristics are "warm" and "cold." (For more on this, take the quiz on page 10.) We tend not to like people who come across as cold, and we gravitate toward warmer people. The lesson? Turn up the heat if you want to be popular.

do you see what I see?

Generally, individuals have their own internal beliefs about themselves, and we tend to see these beliefs reflected in the eyes of other people, whether the reflection is good, bad, or neutral. Thus, perception can be a self-fulfilling prophecy—for better or for worse. For instance, if you believe you are clever, you will be likely to believe that others think you're clever.

In other words, the relationship is circular: We see what we believe, and the "feedback" as we interpret it confirms and bolsters our beliefs.

Do You See Yourself as Others See You?

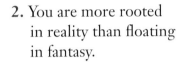

1. You are described as a giving person.

   True   *False*

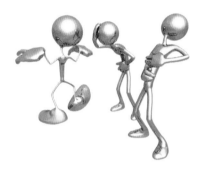

2. You are more rooted in reality than floating in fantasy.

   True   *False*

3. Your friends would say (or have said) that you are calm rather than dramatic.

   True   *False*

4. You have been told that you are kind and compassionate.

   True   *False*

5. You must straighten crooked pictures, and you like absolute neatness.

   True   *False*

6. Your friends and coworkers laugh at your jokes and witticisms.

   True   *False*

7. You have a great laugh.

   True   *False*

8. Being gorgeous is not particularly important to you.

   True   *False*

9. You handle the ups and downs in life without getting overly frustrated.

   True   *False*

Do You See Yourself as Others See You?

10. You can see the silver lining in most storm clouds.

    True   *False*

11. You have been described as friendly and affectionate.

    True   *False*

12. Your friends say they can depend on you when you give your word.

    True   *False*

13. You have been compared to a kitten—playful and mischievous.

    True   *False*

14. You have been told that you are creative and imaginative.

    True   *False*

15. You are loyal to your friends—and they have said so.

    True   *False*

16. You are responsible about paying your own way.

    True   *False*

17. You are curious about the world, and it is reflected in how you spend your time.

    True   *False*

18. You are adventurous and enjoy exploring with your friends.

    True   *False*

19. You are good at your job, and it shows.

    True   *False*

20. You have been told that you are tolerant and are not judgmental.

    True   *False*

Do You See Yourself as Others See You?

Scoring

The statements in this quiz reflect characteristics that we generally admire in others. The more points you tallied, the more you are probably liked, admired, and respected. Don't be distressed if your score is not as high as you would like—now that you know how others perceive you, you can evolve if you try.

Give yourself **1 point** for each "true" response. Tally your score and find your profile below.

0–8 points
More Cold than Hot
You don't give off as many of the positive warm-and-fuzzies as you could. To be certain that you are not being too tough on yourself, ask your friends to answer these questions about you and compare their answers to yours. If they jibe, you may want to make some changes. Or you may be perfectly happy with yourself as you are—and that's okay too. Now that you know how you're perceived, the choice is yours.

9–15 points
Room Temperature
You are highly thought of in quite a few areas. No one is perfect, but you have a generally strong reputation. If you want to tweak your public persona, you won't have far to go. You are doing quite well.

16–20 points
More Hot than Cold
You are probably well respected, admired, and liked. Since you are quite popular, you may be content to continue doing what works so very well for you. There's always room for improvement, though, so you may choose to make those few adjustments and continue to grow. Congratulations: People like you are exceptionally rare. When you look in your mirror tomorrow morning, you will see what everyone else sees. That is a good thing.

seeing is believing

To be certain you scored this quiz fairly, ask your friends for their input!

Can You Decode Body Language?

When we communicate with others, only a very small part of our message is verbal; the bulk is "spoken" by tone, volume, how we accent our words, and our body language. If you consider yourself a sensitive, intuitive, and perceptive person, you probably read body language quite well without even consciously thinking about it. Your subconscious is on guard and paying strict attention. (Are you intuitive? See page 36.)

(Are you intuitive? See page 36.)

❝I speak two languages: Body and English.❞

—*Mae West*

When you meet someone you find attractive, your observation skills may take a backseat to the excitement and interest that flood your brain. Because of this, you may need to pay closer attention. Look for signs of truthfulness, sincerity, and compassion.

Are the eyes really the window to the soul? If you're a talented observer and know what to look for, yes, you can spot some lies—but not all. When lie-detecting, watch for the very first response: Their facial expression, the look in their eyes, or the first thing they say is probably the most reliable clue of all. If you tend to miss the signs and find out later that things weren't quite what you thought they were, don't worry. You can increase your body language–reading skills quite easily, by exploring nonverbal communication and practicing what you learn.

Can You Decode Body Language?

Do you speak the language?

Some of these questions have more than one plausible response. Choose the one (or more) response that feels right to you.

1. You have gone out to dinner with your spouse, who is across the table from you, sitting stiffly in the chair with arms crossed. You instinctively know that crossed arms and erect posture mean:

   a. Spouse is sitting too close to the walk-in freezer.

   b. Spouse is miffed and guarded.

   c. Spouse is shy and reserved.

   d. Spouse is bored and drowsy.

2. You have just spotted an incredibly attractive guy or gal in line at your neighborhood food store. They make eye contact with you and don't quickly look away. You perceive that this person might be:

   a. Aggressive and quite possibly dangerous.

   b. Interested in you.

   c. Extremely nearsighted and attempting to determine if you are friend or foe.

   d. Sleepwalking.

3. While interviewing an applicant to be your child's new nanny, you ask her who she worked for five years ago. Before answering, she looks up and to the right. You have a hunch:

   a. Nanny is not really paying attention.

   b. Nanny is checking out the room.

   c. Nanny is making something up.

   d. Nanny is probably telling the truth.

Can You Decode Body Language?

4. You enjoy volunteering on Saturday mornings at the library. A teenage girl walks up to the counter and hands you her library card and the newest *Twilight* book. When you remind her that she hasn't returned the first book in the series yet, she tells you, "I did not lose *Twilight*. My dog Spike devoured it." Your instinct says:

   a. You do not want to meet Spike.

   b. This girl is not being truthful.

   c. This girl gets her feelings hurt easily.

   d. This girl probably wants to be a veterinarian.

5. You are interviewing for a new job. You arrived on time, you are dressed appropriately, and you answered questions with confidence and skill. Yet your gut feeling is telling you that you won't get the job. Why?

   a. The interviewer maintained a distance and did not make eye contact.

   b. The interviewer was dressed all in black.

   c. The interviewer took a long phone call during the interview.

   d. The interviewer kept calling you by the wrong name.

6. You and your sweetie recently called it quits, and then last night you saw your ex walking briskly down the street with head erect and arms swinging. You perceived this to mean:

   a. Ex-sweetie's self-confidence is high; he or she has probably moved on.

   b. Ex-sweetie is searching for you.

   c. Ex-sweetie is on the prowl.

   d. Ex-sweetie is simply getting some exercise—it means nothing.

7. You are very proud of your intuition and your ability to read people. You are certain that at least one of the following is absolutely true.

   a. If someone is lying, his or her eyes dart or look down.

   b. People who sweat when you question them are lying.

   c. People with high foreheads are unusually intelligent.

   d. People who weep at movies are emotional train wrecks.

Can You Decode Body Language?

8. You just confronted your main squeeze about why he or she didn't show up for your date last night. Your temper sparks when:

   a. Main Squeeze walks around the room with hands clasped behind back.

   b. Main Squeeze sneezes—three times.

   c. Main Squeeze scratches head.

   d. Main Squeeze laughs and says you worry too much.

9. You are on a blind date with someone who seems absolutely fabulous—smart, funny, gorgeous, witty... the list goes on. However, your gut tells you to dump the date when you notice:

   a. Contradictions in statements.

   b. Incongruence in speech and facial expression.

   c. Eyeing other people when he or she thinks you aren't looking.

   d. He or she keeps dropping their napkin or tying their shoelaces.

10. You have just begun a new job and you are anticipating meeting your new coworkers. Your "bad news" antennae come up when one of your team members:

   a. Sits with back straight, hands in lap.

   b. Sits with legs straight, hands clasped behind neck.

   c. Sits with legs crossed and foot keeping time with music (there is no music).

   d. Stands with hands on hips, feet planted firmly far apart.

Answers

1. (b) Your spouse's crossed arms and stiff posture could be telling you he or she is feeling miffed and guarded. Unless, of course, you really are sitting too close to the walk-in freezer—people often cross their arms for warmth.

2. (b) Lucky you: This stranger is interested in more than the fresh produce and vitamin supplements. Prolonged eye contact generally signifies interest.

3. (d) If she looks up and to the right that probably means she is trying to remember the answer to your question. If she had looked up and to the *left*, it could have meant she was fabricating an answer.

Can You Decode Body Language?

4. (b) People who want to sound particularly convincing often avoid contractions. If you noticed that she said "I *did not*" rather than "I *didn't*," you would be right to be dubious about the fate of the book. (Of course, it could be that she just likes to speak formally.)

5. (a, c, and d) Your gut is probably right; it's not likely that you will get a job offer from this interviewer. Three behaviors showed a definite lack of interest: answering her phone, avoiding eye contact, and forgetting your name.

6. (a) A brisk pace with head held high is a sign of confidence and probably a cheery mood. It appears your ex has moved on.

7. (a and b) An individual who is lying might very well avoid eye contact and begin perspiring, but don't start calling foul just yet—these behaviors can indicate other things as well. Though it would appear to make sense, a high forehead does not necessarily mean high intelligence or a large brain. Also, most of us, if we are willing to admit to it, have cried at the movies at one time or another—being emotional or easily moved does not equal "train wreck."

8. (a and d) Walking with hands clasped behind the back shows annoyance and perceived superiority. You would have picked up on that immediately. Also, laughing and discounting your worry was flat-out disrespectful. Not smart, Main Squeeze!

9. (a, b, and c) Your blind date is bad news. Contradicting oneself and being incongruent are signs that your date may be a lemon. And eyeing others while on a date with you speaks volumes about sensitivity—or lack thereof.

10. (d) Hands on hips and feet firmly planted does not bode well for you. The good news is the other behaviors are friendly enough, so you probably have a few allies in the room.

CHAPTER 3
THE LANGUAGE OF LOVE

Yes, all the world loves a lover. The language of love is universal. Even if we don't understand the words, we cannot mistake the tenderness, the twinkling eyes, and the soft glow of amore. Romance is multifaceted: It is your beliefs, dreams, and expectations about love.

In this chapter you can discover if you are a talented flirt. Flirting can come in handy, and it's oh, so much fun. Test your sexuality—just how hot are you? Discover whether you bring out the best in your lover and, if not, how you can increase your score.

How do you know when it's time to let go and move on? Learn how to identify a robust, healthy romance and how to recognize the signs that your relationship is over. Identify the traits you look for in a dream date, and discover what's most important to you in a mate.

The quizzes in this chapter will get your motor running.

Are You a Flirt?

It's not all about fluttering your eyelashes and tossing back your hair: Flirting is a competitive game played by both sexes, and it has a long and honorable history in the evolution and continuation of our species.

It would be impossible to begin a romance without some amount of flirting to get the ball rolling. To keep flirting at its paramount, most accomplished level, everyone involved should understand the rules of engagement. If you are going to flirt at the level of flirters extraordinaire, just remember: Coquetry can quickly turn into a sticky mess if the object of your attention thinks your intentions are altar-serious when actually you are only practicing.

Flirting can be completely innocent—a form of subtle (or not so subtle) flattery that everyone loves. However, if you're flirting for a serious romantic advantage you need serious artillery. As Mae West, the vamp of all vamps, explained, "It's not what I do, but the way I do it. It's not what I say, but the way I say it." Ms. West reached the epitome of the flirting art; her phenomenal style paired sultry wit with steamy body language.

Are You a Flirt?

Do you have what it takes to charm with the best of them?

How well do these statements match your style? Put a checkmark in the corresponding box.

	Never	Sometimes	Always
1. I dress for flirting success in clothes that complement my body and style.	❏	❏	❏
2. My body language says approachable (arms not folded, a great smile) and confident (head high, laid-back cool).	❏	❏	❏
3. If I see someone gorgeous I don't sit on the sidelines and watch—I sashay or amble over and start a conversation.	❏	❏	❏
4. I can flatter with a lusty laugh or a cute giggle.	❏	❏	❏
5. I use my eyes to charm.	❏	❏	❏
6. If the object of my attention appears interested, I occasionally touch his or her arm, hand, or shoulder.	❏	❏	❏
7. I have wit and humor, and I use them as weapons to wow.	❏	❏	❏
8. I remember his or her name and use it often as we get acquainted.	❏	❏	❏
9. I have perfected my sidelong glance, coupled with a sweet, lopsided smile.	❏	❏	❏
10. I have a charmingly tousled bit of hair hanging over my forehead.	❏	❏	❏

Are You a Flirt?

Scoring

Give yourself **0 points** for each "Never" answer, **1 point** for every "Sometimes," and **2 points** for each "Always."

0–7 points
Finding Your Inner Flirt

Did you know that we are programmed to flirt? Absolutely! Researchers will confirm this scientific fact: You do flirt. Therefore, even if you received a score of "0," it's likely you are more talented and better programmed than you realize. You can increase your score with a little effort. The next time you attend a party or find yourself in a social situation, keep your eye on the belle of the ball. Chances are she's a world-class flirter, so now's a perfect time to pick up some pointers. If the thought of overt flirting makes you retreat into your shell, just be warm and kind and you will do just fine.

8–14 points
Mildly Flirtatious

Researchers call little flirting acts such as a lopsided grin, a touch on the arm, or a toss of the head "contact-readiness" cues. This simple body language suggests that you're prepared to spend fun time with your prey. You've got the moves down, so you really can't flub flirting. Indeed, your score indicates that you are quite talented already. Enhance your prowess or simply enjoy your current robust flirting talent.

15–20 points
Fabulously Flirtatious

You are a champion flirt; obviously, you know all the tricks. You may be one of those lucky individuals who is simply witty and extroverted, and flirting is a side effect of your charismatic personality. (Are you charismatic? Turn to page 132 to find out.) Or you may simply know how and when to turn on the charm. Flirting—for you—is positively effortless.

Does Your Sex Drive Need a Tune-up?

If you have been having terrible "headaches" at bedtime recently, maybe the Romance Grinch is stealing your sex drive. There are all sorts of stealthy monsters that, at one time or another, may hide under the bed and try to stamp out your groove. To be on top of your game, you have to research the monsters and be ready to slay them on sight.

Is maintaining a lively libido at the top of your to-do list? If you are an extraordinarily sexy being you have done your homework and know all of the little extras that enhance your desire. Even more important, you have sought out and destroyed the monsters under the bed.

> **"An intellectual is someone who has found something more interesting than sex."**
> — *Edgar Wallace*

Stop and think for a moment: Where do you focus most of your time and attention? That is the area of your life that you value most highly. Where does your sex life rank? Let's see how dedicated you are to your libido.

Does Your Sex Drive Need a Tune-up?

How lively is your libido?

1. My bedroom is ready for romance (candles, flowers, big comfy bed, plush materials).

   True　　　*False*

2. Get enough exercise? You bet your bippy I do!

   True　　　*False*

3. I (and my lover) are moderate, light, or zero drinkers of alcohol.

   True　　　*False*

4. I gobble up fresh fruits and vegetables, whole grains, and lean meats.

   True　　　*False*

5. I know that mild to severe melancholia can quash my desire for pleasure of all types.

   True　　　*False*

6. When my sizzle fizzles I take the time to figure out why.

   True　　　*False*

7. I am not a worrywart.

   True　　　*False*

8. To stay healthy and sexually robust, I make sure I get seven to nine hours of sleep at night.

   True　　　*False*

9. I believe that Viagra can be the silver bullet for both men and women.

   True　　　*False*

10. I (and/or my lover) take prescription medications, and I have checked the side effects for romance killers.

    True　　　*False*

    (I do not take prescription medication, but I know that it can interfere with my libido.)

Does Your Sex Drive Need a Tune-up?

Scoring

Give yourself **1 point** for each time you answered "true." (In the last question, give yourself **1 point** for either "true" or "I do not take prescription medication.") Doing your research and having the absolutely invaluable information is what counts.

0–3 points
Optimistically Uninformed

You have not yet begun to concern your-self with the flight of libido. Perhaps you are still quite young and it seems like any problem in this department is decades away. (No matter who you are, mojo misalignment can happen at any age. That's just how things work.) You may be optimistic and fun-loving by nature and simply trust that things will turn out well. If so, this cheery attitude will save you a few frown lines, but it will not save your groove. You can learn everything you ever wanted to know about wellness and your libido with a little help from your neigh-borhood bookstore or the Internet. Study time—happy reading.

4–7 points
The Dawning Light

You are beginning to gather information to use if and when the time comes—whenever that may be. Perhaps you have suffered through one or two nights when the sparks did not fly with uninhibited abandon. These things happen. But you believe that one should be prepared. Though you are relatively buoyant, you have found that without oxygen, flames will die out. Realism comes in handy.

8–10 points
Mojo Hero

Obviously you value your love life. In fact, it's probably not a stretch to say you *highly* value your love life, and you plan to keep it in well-oiled, fully functioning condition. It's likely you are committed to achievement in many areas of your life. You are organized and carefully plan your life for success. Your lover is very lucky.

Do You Bring Out the Best in Your Lover?

Each of us has a great deal of personal power. We have power over our behaviors, and we have more power than we sometimes realize over how others respond to us. Unfortunately, sometimes we use that power to try to mold our lover into the person we want him or her to be. Attempts to nag, push, and/or manipulate never work well—in fact, such behavior can damage an otherwise good relationship.

It's a fact that falling in love is chemically induced: When natural chemicals such as serotonin flood the brain, they create a sense of euphoria—the classic "love is blind" state. When the chemical-induced fog begins to clear, we may start to notice some annoying little habits. What might not have bugged you in the beginning may start to drive you crazy. If we approach the problem from high ground— ask for what we want in a positive, caring way, without recriminations—we might actually get it, and this is the key to preserving the relationship.

If you want to bring out the best in your partner, expect the best and model the nurturing behaviors you want to encourage. The magic of self-fulfilling prophecies and loving compassion can do wonders.

> **There isn't time—so brief is life—for bickering, apologies, heartburning, callings to account. There is only time for loving— & but an instant, so to speak, for that.**
>
> —*Mark Twain*

Do You Bring Out the Best in Your Lover?

are you lovely to your lover?

	Not really	Sometimes	All the time
1. I ask for (not demand) what I want.	❏	❏	❏
2. I am willing to do a little friendly give-and-take negotiation.	❏	❏	❏
3. I don't nag, and I don't want to be nagged.	❏	❏	❏
4. I don't try to negotiate when one of us is angry. I wait for a better time.	❏	❏	❏
5. I compliment all of my partner's behaviors that are an "improvement."	❏	❏	❏
6. I recognize my little irritating habits, and that helps me understand my sweetie's minute flaws.	❏	❏	❏
7. I have good communication skills, and I listen with my heart and my mind.	❏	❏	❏
8. I try to focus on the relationship, rather than just my side of an issue.	❏	❏	❏
9. Emotions are contagious, so I try to stay sympathetic and reasonable.	❏	❏	❏
10. I focus on the positives and work with my partner on the changes we want.	❏	❏	❏

Do You Bring Out the Best in Your Lover?

Scoring

Give yourself **1 point** for "Not really," **2 points** for "Sometimes," and **3 points** for "All the time."

10–17 points
Living and Learning

You are not quite the great communicator and negotiator you could be. Perhaps this relationship is new to you and you are still getting up to speed. We all have the ability to bring out the best in others; however, the skills we need—including compromise, positive communication, and the ability to listen with a loving ear—are not necessarily innate. Most of them have to be learned. Don't forget to focus on why you chose your lover and the wonderful qualities he or she has. Directing your attention to this will create an almost miraculous difference in your relationship. Maybe your lover will be encouraged to overlook some of your tiny flaws also. Now that's a good deal.

18–25 points
The Negotiator

You are interested in maintaining a loving relationship, and you are willing to do your part to bring out the best in your lover. Good for you. You are a caring person who doesn't mind going the extra mile. You understand that no one's perfect, and you're realistic about yourself, your partner, and the fleeting life of serotonin in the human body. Perhaps you would like to team up with your lover to resurrect your early nearsighted, yet passionate, relationship. Practice, practice, practice!

26–30 points
The Great Communicator

People notice when you bring out the best in them—honestly. Your lover knows and probably tries to live up to your rosy, optimistic beliefs. Cooperation breeds cooperation, and you appear to be doing a fine job of relating to each other. It's quite possible that you are able to extend these skills to the rest of your life—you may be in a profession that values the very communication skills that make your love life crackle with vitality and optimism. No doubt you also have many devoted friends who are warmed by your sensitive and appreciative nature. Bringing out the best in your friends and loved ones is a very special talent. Enjoy it—they do.

How Healthy Is Your Romance?

"A true man does not need to romance a different girl every night; a true man romances the same girl for the rest of her life."

—*Anu Alas*

Who wouldn't absolutely adore a healthy, robust romance that totally crackles with electricity? If you've been in a relationship for a while, you probably noticed that even the most sizzling romance eventually starts to fade. But don't worry: If you've lost the quiver of passion, you can get it back. If it's on a downward slide, you can halt it in its tracks. And if you've still got it, read on to learn what to do to keep it.

Romances that last are usually between people who genuinely like each other, share common interests, are determined to make their relationship work—and are willing to devote the time and effort needed to make sure that it does. The key to a lasting, passionate romance is commitment to each other and the willingness on both parts to work to keep the flames alive. Romance requires a great expenditure of time and energy—but it's worth it.

The path to your very own Bogie-and-Bacall, Elizabeth Bennet-and-Mr. Darcy, or Carrie Bradshaw-and-Mr. Big love story is fraught with exasperating obstacles. Romances that become legends don't just happen. Long-term relationship survival requires planning and faithful safeguarding.

How Healthy Is Your Romance?

Is your romance hot?

	Uh-uh	Kinda	Uh-huh!
1. I have consciously made my relationship a top priority in my life.	☐	☐	☐
2. I allocate enough special together time to feel connected to my lover.	☐	☐	☐
3. I would say my sizzle level is an 8 or above on a scale of 1 to 10.	☐	☐	☐
4. I actively listen to my partner. (Signs of active listening include leaning forward, paraphrasing, and making eye contact.)	☐	☐	☐
5. I have a structured plan to increase the longevity of my romance.	☐	☐	☐
6. Most of my interactions (at least four out of five) with my lover are positive.	☐	☐	☐
7. When I make important decisions, I consistently consider my lover's best interests as well as my own.	☐	☐	☐
8. I compliment and thank my lover regularly, even for such mundane chores as preparing a meal or taking out the trash.	☐	☐	☐

How Healthy Is Your Romance?

	Uh-uh	Kinda	Uh-huh!
9. I avoid critical or demeaning language.	☐	☐	☐
10. I make a point of saying "I love you" often.	☐	☐	☐
11. Our disagreements are generally structured to be productive rather than verbal free-for-alls.	☐	☐	☐
12. I still, on occasion, try to "wow" my sweetie by slipping into something sexy.	☐	☐	☐
13. I look for ways to keep excitement in my romance, even if it's just mountain climbing. (That chemistry needs revving every once in a while!)	☐	☐	☐
14. I nourish the similar interests that connected us in the early days of our romance.	☐	☐	☐

rejuvenating the romance

There is no real mystery about what causes the snap, crackle, and pop in romance. In fact, scientists are quite certain that chemistry in the brain produces the flulike symptoms typically associated with new love—you can't eat, you can't sleep, you can't concentrate. You can expect these intoxicating brain chemicals to stick around for about one year—probably less. And when the miracle of chemistry begins to fizzle, get ready to begin love-CPR. A forgiving nature, open affection, being a good listener, lots of laughter, unwavering support, and comfy camaraderie are a few of the vital romance rejuvenators.

How Healthy Is Your Romance?

Scoring

Give yourself **0 points** for each "Uh-uh," **1 point** for every "Kinda," and **2 points** for each "Uh-huh!"

0–9 points
Slow Burn

You are still eagerly learning about romance. Good for you! Please go back and look at your "Uh-uh" responses. If you work to turn them into "Uh-huh!" responses, you'll see your romantic score soar.

A strong partner relationship can help improve your health by reducing stress, often helping you to reach your career and life goals. Following the tips on the opposite page will help you turn up the heat *and* increase your success quotient—what a bargain!

10–20 points
Starting to Sizzle

You are doing quite well in the romance department. However, you may want to turn up the sizzle—and who could blame you? You are probably in a satisfying relationship that will withstand the test of time, but it may need some heat. Think about the questions you answered with a disappointing "Uh-uh." Could you strut your stuff closer to an "Uh-huh"? It just may be time to kick things into gear with a huge hug and a wicked wink. Consider taking off on a romantic rendezvous—whether it's a weekend at a bed-and-breakfast or a week on a tropical beach—to ignite a romantic bonfire.

21–28 points
Too Hot to Handle

Hello, hottie. Is it hot in your house, or is that just you? You and your sweetie have found a relationship that works for you, and you are wise not to take it for granted. You probably value important couple occasions, sweet little surprises for no apparent reason, and the comfortable bliss you feel when you share quiet moments with the one who absolutely curls your toes. Did you know that just holding your lover's hand can reduce your pulse rate? Of course, it can also start your heart racing . . . in a good way.

How Healthy Is Your Romance?

keeping things hot, hot, hot

Have at least one romantic dinner a week— just the two of you.

Hold hands when you walk.

Keep the sizzle alive with exciting new adventures.

Give little gifts and surprises.

Take time for stimulating conversations.

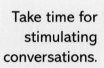

Decorate your bedroom as a romantic retreat.

Pamper your sweetie with a warm bubble bath and romantic music.

Send sweet e-mails.

Hide romantic notes in pockets, dresser drawers, and lunch boxes.

Are You Ready for a New Relationship?

Breakups are painful, no doubt about it. So how do you know if you're ready to move on to a new relationship? The better question may be: "Are you ready to move on—at all?" One of the

> **"Pain is inevitable. Suffering is optional."**
> —*Anonymous*

most important considerations when you take your first wary steps toward a new relationship is: "Is my heart free to love again?" It isn't easy to overcome the searing pain of a lost love. Most of us have been there at some point in our life, and we desperately hope we never go there again.

You've done your "heartsick" homework. You confided in your friends, you shed gallons of tears, you listened to hours of sappy love songs, and you have analyzed every moment of your tattered relationship.

Are you ready to stand up and sing "I Will Survive?"

Are You Ready for a New Relationship?

Has your heart healed?

1. How often do everyday situations and places remind you of your former love?

   a. Every day.

   b. Several times a week—darn it.

   c. Not more than once a week. See? I am getting over it! *(Bite tongue.)*

   d. Never.

2. When you are reminded of your ex, how hard does the emotional bus hit you?

   a. Knee-bucklingly bad.

   b. I see a few stars, then I grind my teeth.

   c. Moderately. Okay, so I have to catch my breath, but I really am getting over it—I swear. *(Mop brow.)*

   d. Now let me see, what was his (her) name?

3. Do you have a plan to recapture your former sweetie?

   a. Yes, and it's as detailed as the battle plan for the Normandy invasion.

   b. Only when I dream—oops, that would be a nightmare.

   c. No—and I didn't have my ex in mind when I bought that killer outfit. *(Yeah, so it's his/her favorite color? So what?)*

   d. Not even a passing thought.

4. Do you go out of your way to "accidentally" bump into your ex?

   a. I hang out at all of my ex's favorite spots.

   b. I see my ex everywhere—only, it's always someone else. Not that I want to see that skunk anyway.

   c. If I just happen to be in close proximity, that doesn't mean I'm a stalker. *(Heart pounds.)*

   d. You must be kidding! I am totally too busy.

5. Is your ex's contact info still programmed into your phone?

   a. Everything: e-mail, work phone, home phone, cell phone, mom's house . . . .

   b. I don't seem to be able to get rid of everything, *yet.*

   c. It's imprinted on my brain—not that I care. *(Stomach tightens.)*

   d. I deleted it all a long time ago.

Are You Ready for a New Relationship?

6. A few weeks after the final blowup you were:

   a. Eating fudge and bursting into spontaneous tears every so often.

   b. Spending time out with friends, hoping to bump into my ex—so I could ignore him.

   c. Fine. I was fine. And I'm still fine. And I will be fine. *(Is it hot in here?)*

   d. Meeting lots of new people, enjoying my life.

7. Has your love turned to anger?

   a. No, I'm too busy trying to smile through quivering lips.

   b. Angry? I sure am. Truthfully? I still have painful moments.

   c. Angry? Why would I be angry? *(Heart pounds.)*

   d. What is there to be angry about?

8. You heard that your ex is dating one of your friends. How do you feel?

   a. I am devastated.

   b. I'm going to call my friend right now—I'm ready to hear some explaining! Darn, why do I care?

   c. Excuse me, my ex? What ex? *(Where are my antacids?)*

   d. That's cool. I hope they're having fun—I am.

9. When you think about your lost love, what do you remember most?

   a. Every tiny detail.

   b. A warm, loving smile—the jerk.

   c. Nothing. I've blocked it all out. *(My neck is stiff.)*

   d. The good times—a few special memories that make me smile.

10. You just received a surprise e-mail from your ex asking how you are doing. How would you respond?

   a. I am miserable and I miss you. Let's get together and talk about us.

   b. First reflex—happy surprise… second, you have your nerve—writing to me.

   c. You don't exist—I can't possibly reply! *(My head hurts.)*

   d. Why would I reply?

Are You Ready for a New Relationship?

Scoring

More "a" answers
Need a Little Push

You are carrying burdensome emotional baggage. Your ex is still very much a part of your life—in your mind. It's possible that your breakup was recent and you have not had time to gain the emotional and intellectual distance you need to heal. But if your relationship ended months (or even years) ago, it's time to get back out there, open yourself up to new experiences, and begin to recover your groove. (Need a little push? Download Gloria Gaynor's "I Will Survive," and turn up the volume!) For now, pull up your bootstraps, tighten your belt, and repeat after me: I *will* survive. Keep up this attitude, and before long you'll be ready to toss your battered emotional baggage in the closest dumpster.

More "b" answers
Getting There

You have given up much of your idealization and moved on to "what a jerk." Your anger is snaking around the edges, which can be a good thing; anger is a sign that you're healing and beginning to move on. Congratulate yourself for passing the first dead-romance hurdle, and hang on to this edge of anger; it will energize you. It takes time to process the hurt, and fluctuating between caring and anger is normal. When you quit waffling and realize you're not angry anymore, you're there.

More "c" answers
Time to Move On

No doubt about it, you are in the river of denial. It is okay to be sad at times. Accept the tears when they come, and then let it go. Once you admit that you're hurt and give yourself permission to cry, you may wallow in your misery for a little while. And then it's time to move on. Focus on your future—where you want to be rather than where you were. You have plenty of options ahead of you—don't forget that. Adopt the motto: "I am a totally fabulous catch," and start believing it.

More "d" answers
You Made It

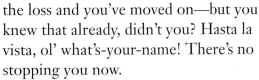

Wow! What a warrior! Your relationship flamed out; the ashes are cold and gray. This quiz is confirmation that you survived the loss and you've moved on—but you knew that already, didn't you? Hasta la vista, ol' what's-your-name! There's no stopping you now.

Do You Pick Losers?

Have you ever fallen for someone charming, witty, and gorgeous, and then—several heartaches and heartbreaks later—realized he or she was totally bad news? Do you choose self-involved jerks and imagine a blissful future together? You may even spot his or her flaws from the get-go, but you think you can change them.

Quick, call the doctor: You may have a case of *loserinfectionitis.* What, you've never heard of this disease? If you're a nurturing, hopeless romantic, you have a high chance of catching it. If you give more to the relationship than you get out of it*, if you often wonder where he or she is, or if you have heard one excuse too many—you have the symptoms.

> **❝Before I met my husband, I'd never fallen in love. I'd stepped in it a few times.❞**
>
> —Rita Rudner

be Web wary

In the 21st century there's a new twist in the dating game: online dating sites. If Internet lizards have preyed on you, please know— you are not alone. Well-scripted opening lines and boldfaced whoppers are remarkably easy to post. Obviously, everything—every single word—is suspect in e-mails between perfect strangers. Watch out for—and delete—the losers.

Fortunately, there is a cure. Be true to yourself first; pay attention to behaviors, not words (bad-news guys or gals talk a great game, but they don't follow through); when you say "no," mean it; and, perhaps most important, get an unbiased perspective from your friends or a professional.

Take our Are You a Giver or a Taker? quiz on page 45 to learn more about this.

Do You Pick Losers?

Are you a loser magnet?

1. My heart goes *thump, thump* when I meet someone with an aura of danger—how exciting!

   True   *False*

2. I feel a sexy little sizzle when I see a hot, toned body.

   True   *False*

3. I love a guy or gal who oozes self-confidence from every pore.

   True   *False*

4. I want to be pursued by someone with lusty determination.

   True   *False*

5. I absolutely melt in the face of devastating charm.

   True   *False*

6. I love to nurture the sensitive and downtrodden who are trying to find themselves.

   True   *False*

7. If the relationship is rocky, I search for ways to make my sweetie happier.

   True   *False*

8. I am turned on by dominant alpha personalities.

   True   *False*

Do You Pick Losers?

9. The strong and silent type intrigues me. I welcome the challenge to get my mate to open up.

True   *False*

10. I think smoldering anger is a sign of passion.

True   *False*

11. The more fabulous and attractive someone is, the more attention and admiration they deserve.

True   *False*

12. When a date makes all of the decisions, it means they are strong and resolute.

True   *False*

13. Lovers who leave a long line of broken hearts behind them simply have not found the right mate.

True   *False*

14. My friends and family have reservations about my sweetie only because they don't know him (her) like I do.

True   *False*

Do You Pick Losers?

Scoring

Give yourself **1 point** for each "true" you marked. A low score means you're infection-free. A high score indicates a serious, though not fatal, case of *loserinfectionitis.*

0–4 points
Healthy Immunity

Your antibodies have this one covered: It looks like you're immune to *loserinfectionitis.* There's no such thing as a lovable loser in your book; when it comes to losers, your motto is "Leave 'em, don't love 'em!" Losers are by nature insincere and egotistical, and lucky for you your immune system repels them. You are not susceptible to superficial or worryingly unstable characters.

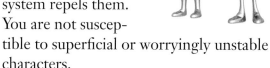

5–9 points
Under the Weather

You're a bit under the weather, but don't worry; with a little rest and some TLC you'll be better in no time. Take a break from anyone who might infect you: If someone has the symptoms of a loser (including, but not limited to: too good to be true, dishonest, aggressive, intolerant, or frightened silly by commitment), steer clear. Treat yourself the way you deserve to be treated, and concentrate on finding someone who will do the same. You've already shown you recognize the type to look out for. Just remember to avoid exposure to this type, and you'll be fine.

10–14 points
Diagnosis: A Nasty Case of Loserinfectionitis

You've got a bug you just can't shake, and its symptoms are severe. If you are frequently unhappy in your relationships, if you feel you're carrying the entire burden for making them work, and/or if you feel unappreciated—you may have been bitten. Don't worry: *loserinfectionitis* is not fatal, and you can expect a full recovery if you follow the doctor's orders (page 86). This might require a quarantine until you build up your immunity, because it can be almost impossible to avoid losers: Some are so darn charged with animal magnetism, charm, and/or charisma, there should be a law against it. (Speaking of animal magnetism and charisma, see our quizzes on pages 118 and 132.)

Who Is Your Dream Date?

Attraction is a personal matter. Someone who makes your knees weaken, your heart flutter, and your pulse race may leave your best friend entirely unmoved. What, or rather who, rings your bell depends on your personality and unique proclivities. You may be pulled in by a beautiful face—you look for the shape of their head, the way their lips turn up when they smile, sexy eyes, or a kissable mouth. Others are more interested in a buff and well-muscled body and six-pack abs. Some people are tuned into a melodious voice; others use height as a gauge; and some are turned on by intelligence and wit.

"There's nothing half so sweet in life as love's young dream."
—*Clement C. Moore*

We've compiled a superstar list of mega-hot choices. Whatever your personality yearns for, it's a good bet you'll find it here.

Who lights your fire... and why?

Choose from the list—it's okay if more than one of these charmers sounds appealing. No one ever said attraction is limited to just one type.

MAN, OH MAN, I MUST BE DREAMING!

1. Jon Bon Jovi
2. Taye Diggs
3. Paul Newman
4. Brad Pitt
5. Elvis Presley
6. Johnny Depp
7. George Clooney
8. Tiger Woods
9. Keith Urban
10. Prince William

Turn to page 92 for a list of lovely ladies.

Who Is Your Dream Date?

1. You're turned on by sexy vocals, a hot rhythm guitar, tousled hair, and a sexy smile. You're looking for someone who's been around the block and knows how to have fun—but also knows how to keep it real and is not afraid of commitment.

2. You're attracted to men who can turn your head with a buff body, melt your heart with a killer smile, and catch your ear with pitch-perfect vocals. A well-rounded talent, good humor, and smarts seal the deal for you, because you want the total package.

3. You're looking for a real class act. You set the bar high, and while a chiseled face and mesmerizing eyes may draw you in, a man's got to display stand-up character, a big heart, and boundless generosity to keep you coming back for more.

4. Classic good looks, a good-natured smile, and eyes you could get lost in will turn your head every time, but looks aren't everything to you. (Though they're a definite plus!) You're seeking someone who cares about others and is willing to put his money where his mouth is. You're probably also looking for someone who's ready to settle down and, eh-hem, start a family.

5. Cocky. Charismatic. Sensual. Larger than life. Let's face it, you're powerless against the lure of colossal sex appeal. Bedroom eyes and a knowing grin are like catnip to you, but you've learned that sometimes this attraction can lead you toward heartbreak hotel.

6. Dashing, dark-eyed, and a little broody may ignite a slow burn in you. You like passion that sizzles under the surface, and your dream date is a cool cat who commands attention but doesn't flaunt his looks or clout in a bid to seek the spotlight.

7. Twinkling eyes and sexy laugh lines are the signs of a mischievous sense of humor—and nothing's more charming to you than a guy who makes you laugh. And if he's easy on the eyes, all the better! Self-confidence and poise are sexy, and a man who's not afraid to stand up for causes near and dear to his heart is the man for you.

8. You're ready to tee it up with a man with a competitive edge. Charisma and self-confidence are the name of the game—you're drawn to a fellow who radiates success, whether in his personal or

Who Is Your Dream Date?

professional life. Success and popularity are par for the course for the man who will capture your heart, and he'll beat out the competition every time.

9. Your ideal man wears his heart on his sleeve, and it looks good on him! Rugged good looks and a casual sense of style sing an irresistible tune—you want someone who's sensitive and romantic and not afraid to show it.

10. You really go for the gold. Golden boys, that is: with blond locks, blue eyes, flashing white teeth, and youthful energy. Not every man is a prince by blood, but you're looking to nab a prince of a man.

GIRL TALK

1. Beyoncé Knowles
2. Angelina Jolie
3. Reese Witherspoon
4. Danica Patrick

5. Jennifer Aniston
6. Marilyn Monroe
7. Tyra Banks

8. Drew Barrymore
9. Serena Williams
10. Victoria Beckham

1. Confident, charismatic, successful… your ideal woman is the complete package. Passionate about her own personal and professional ventures, this is a lady who won't feel the need to crowd in on your successes—she's too busy enjoying her own! You are looking for a woman who is steadfast and true—a woman who is, in a word, irreplaceable.

2. A woman with a "bad girl" image but a heart of gold is what really turns you on. You enjoy all the excitement life has to offer when taking the road less traveled, but ultimately believe that we are put here on this earth to do good. A rebel *with* a cause—now that's the idea! Start a family she may—but settle down, never!

3. You're looking for a partner who's as sweet as she looks. You appreciate a gentle, yet mischievous, nature and a quality sense of humor. Add intelligence and a solid cultural background, and you've found your perfect mate!

Who Is Your Dream Date?

4. A woman with an adventurous streak really gets your motor running. You're looking for a beauty who's not only able to hold her own while you live life in the fast lane, but is competitive enough to race you to the finish. She's just like "one of the guys"—but a whole lot sexier.

5. You're looking for a woman who's real. Down-to-earth and genuine, with a girl-next-door kind of charm that belies her sexiness, your ideal partner is a sweetheart who radiates goodwill and will be your loyal friend. Lovely and graceful with a sunny personality, she also has—and enjoys—a sense of humor.

6. Your ideal woman is the classic bombshell. Gorgeous, sensuous, curvaceous—she is the very definition of pure, feminine sex appeal. You are drawn to a woman with an aura of innocence and vulnerability about her—you are a true romantic at heart, a knight in search of a princess to rescue.

7. A commanding presence and fierce beauty demand your attention, but the woman who catches your eye must have a self-awareness that goes way beyond skin-deep. She is compassionate and thoughtful, yet capable of brutal honesty, and you appreciate that. She exudes confidence and strength—the very picture of empowerment.

8. Sunshine on a cloudy day—that's what your girl is! An eternal optimist and free-spirited sweetie, she's a person everyone (you included!) can't help but love to be around. A sunny good nature is attractive to you; naiveté is not. Cheerfulness is contagious, and if beneath the happy demeanor is a hint of unpredictability, that's all the better for you.

9. A woman with a competitive edge is the perfect match for you. Living an active lifestyle is a top priority, and your partner must be able to keep up. This woman has goals, and she knows how to achieve them. (To you, that's very sexy.) Of course, it doesn't hurt that her lifestyle lends her a perfect athlete's physique, either.

10. Posh, poised, and with a signature pout—all eyes are on your dream date, and that's just the way you like it! You are drawn to a woman who is comfortable in the spotlight. No matter that she's a bit high-maintenance; you'd love a chance to spoil your very own stunning goddess.

CHAPTER 4

ALL IN A DAY'S WORK

On average, Americans work more hours than European workers and are less likely to take vacation time. Thus—you may spend more time with coworkers than you do with family members and friends! Are you an awesome employee? A good coworker? How do you know if you're living up to your full potential?

Many people have become workaholics. Perhaps you aren't sure how much work is too much. On the other hand, rather than compulsively pressing for success, do you talk yourself into failure? If the running dialogue in our heads is positive and "pro-self" we are likely to succeed; if not, we have a major hurdle to overcome. Learn the simple secret to successful self-talk.

Procrastinators put off until tomorrow what they could do today. Procrastinating takes a toll on your career achievements and your health. Or, perhaps you excel at winning—no matter the cost. Learn the pros and cons of the competitive spirit.

The quizzes in this chapter will help you find your path to success.

Are You an Awesome Employee?

What are companies looking for when they hire a new employee? What makes a five-star worker? Naturally, a lot depends on the job description. Nonetheless, there are some basic qualities and characteristics that are highly sought-after by the corporate world, law enforcement, government agencies, and small businesses.

"Always do more than is required of you."
—*General George S. Patton*

If you were a hiring manager, what would you seek in the ideal employee? You would probably look for many of the same qualities valued by HR departments around the globe: No doubt you would choose someone who is pleasant, cooperative, a team player, dependable, intelligent, self-motivated, consistent, enthusiastic, optimistic, with a "get 'er done" attitude; someone who wants to grow as an employee, follows through on tasks, and is a good communicator. How do you measure up?

funny business

A good sense of humor is a great attribute in an employee. Life is entirely too short to be blind to the irony and humor in all situations, especially work. If you can laugh at something, including yourself, you will diffuse many stressful situations. A cheerful, optimistic individual with a keen sense of humor is worth his or her weight in gold.

Are You an Awesome Employee?

Are you workin' it?

How well do these statements match your workstyle? Put a checkmark in the appropriate box.

	Rarely	Sometimes	Often
1. I arrive at work early.	❑	❑	❑
2. I ask for more responsibility.	❑	❑	❑
3. I avoid excessive chitchatting with my coworkers.	❑	❑	❑
4. I am cheerful.	❑	❑	❑
5. I go out of my way to help my employer and coworkers.	❑	❑	❑
6. I am a problem-solver.	❑	❑	❑
7. I finish assignments on schedule.	❑	❑	❑
8. I am enthusiastic about my work.	❑	❑	❑
9. I am a team player.	❑	❑	❑
10. I try to get to know my coworkers.	❑	❑	❑
11. I dress to succeed in my work environment.	❑	❑	❑
12. I go the extra mile—above and beyond what is expected of me.	❑	❑	❑
13. I strive for excellence.	❑	❑	❑
14. I am competitive in a healthy way. (I want to win, but I am a good sport if I do not.)	❑	❑	❑
15. I have a clear idea of my goals and a plan to achieve them.	❑	❑	❑

Are You an Awesome Employee?

Scoring

Give yourself **1 point** for "Rarely," **2 points** for "Sometimes," and **3 points** for "Often." Tally your points and look for your profile below.

15–25 points
The Free Spirit

The corporate world may not be for you—it seems you're more of a free spirit who enjoys variety and the freedom of independent pursuits. You are probably not in a 9:00–5:00 job; or, if you are, it may not be a harmonious fit for your personality. Much depends on which questions you answered "rarely" to. The last three questions are more about you as an individual rather than as an employee. If you answered "often" to those questions, you have what it takes to be successful, though perhaps not in a traditional career role. No matter what your score, you can be as successful as your heart desires. Success is a nebulous concept—and you are the only one who can keep score for yourself.

26–35 points
Seeking Your Niche

You may not be a people person, or you may prefer a more independent environment. People skills are a huge determinate in finding the perfect career fit. If your people skills don't match your career, you could feel disgruntled and frustrated. Evaluate your personal attributes to help you find your niche in the workplace. If you're doing work that keeps your blood pulsing everyday, you're rocking. Moderate job performance in a career you love can be preferable to wild success in a career you merely tolerate.

36–45 points
Awesome Employee

You just may be the "ideal" employee. Congratulations! You have the characteristics that employers would kill for. But keep in mind that being the ideal employee does not necessarily guarantee career satisfaction. Ask yourself if you are happy in your profession. If you're not, think about taking your exceptional employee skills to a job that instills a twinkle in your eye and a spring in your step.

Are You a Workaholic?

Some people view the workaholic personality as self-sacrificing and noble; others think it is selfish and self-absorbed. A more likely description is that this personality type is somewhere between these two extremes—an individual who is sincerely dedicated to his or her career. Many of the world's wondrous inventions and discoveries are the by-products of zealous workaholics. For example, according to historians, Thomas Edison's entire staff worked frantically—around the clock, in fact. And you may have noticed that today we are not sitting in the dark.

Is work really "work" if you love what you do? There is no absolute good or bad in work habits. If you are happy, and your relationships are rich and rewarding, then you are doing what is right for you. However, problems may arise if a harried worker is more enthusiastic about his or her career than about loved ones, friends, coworkers, and leisure activities.

> **"The work will wait while you show the child the rainbow, but the rainbow won't wait while you do the work."**
>
> —*Anonymous*

hands off!

Workaholics are frequently perfectionists. They may feel that they must guard their professional tasks closely; they don't trust anyone else to do them.

Are You a Workaholic?

Do you burn the midnight oil?

Please choose the response that most closely represents your work philosophy.

1. My normal workweek is:

    a. Less than 40 hours

    b. 40 to 45 hours

    c. More than 45 hours

2. My attitude about delegating work is:

    a. The more the merrier.

    b. I welcome competent help.

    c. Really, I think I had better do this myself. . . .

3. My opinion about having fun is:

    a. You can't overdo a good thing.

    b. To everything there is a season.

    c. Work, work, work, work—before play (if there's time).

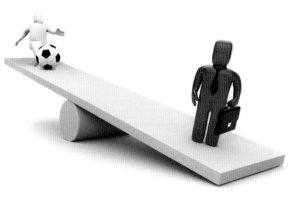

4. My philosophy about work is:

    a. I like work, "particularly when performed, quietly and unobtrusively, by someone else." (Barbara Ehrenreich)

    b. I give my all for my job—9 to 5, five days a week, with all holidays off.

    c. Work—exceptionally hard work—moves mountains.

5. My sweetie would say this about my work:

    a. "You never allow your work to interfere with what is important—our fun."

    b. "You work hard, but you're there when I need you."

    c. "What's your name again?"

6. My favorite reading material is:

    a. Fun stuff—hobby and special interest publications, Internet blogs

    b. Newspapers, best sellers, Internet news

    c. Career-related news, journals, Web sites

Are You a Workaholic?

7. I typically leave work:

   a. As soon as the bell rings.

   b. As soon as I finish the absolutely-must-be-done tasks.

   c. When the cleanup crew leaves.

8. What makes my heart pound and my pulse race?

   a. Are you kidding? My sweetie.

   b. My anniversary, my kid's smile, playing Frisbee with my dog.

   c. Recognition by my professional peers—a "perfect" conclusion to a project.

9. When family celebrations conflict with work, my attitude is:

   a. Work will still be there tomorrow.

   b. I have missed a celebration on a few occasions—I can count the times on one hand.

   c. I can't possibly get away—you just can't imagine how busy I am—I'll try to make it next time.

10. My legacy will be:

   a. "I don't want to achieve immortality through my work... I want to achieve it through not dying." (Woody Allen)

   b. My family.

   c. The same as Thomas Edison: my bright ideas and successes.

Are You a Workaholic?

Scoring

More "a" answers
Laid-back

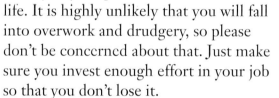

You are definitely not a workaholic, and your self-concept is not defined by your career. You are a laid-back, live-for-today, fun-loving romantic who invests enthusiastically and heavily in your personal life. It is highly unlikely that you will fall into overwork and drudgery, so please don't be concerned about that. Just make sure you invest enough effort in your job so that you don't lose it.

More "b" answers
Reasonably Invested

You are intensely interested in both your career and in your life—and fortunately you realize they are not necessarily one and the same. You want to get the job done well and you are proud of your work, but your core enthusiasm is dedicated to your family and your buds. Under stressful circumstances you may show signs of workaholism, and that's okay—for a little while. You take pride in a job well done, but you know when to say when. It wouldn't hurt to give your travel agent a call and get a vacation on the books.

More "c" answers
Enthusiastically Dedicated

Your career is exceptionally important to you. It provides rewards, intellectual stimulation, and a sense of purpose. Naturally, you spend much of your time thinking, planning, and strategizing about work—even when you are not physically at the workplace. With so much dedication, work can become who you are, not what you do. Even if your job itself is not a stressful one, you may have made it such by attempting to maintain your commitment to work while struggling to keep the home fires burning. There are certain negatives associated with such devotion, such as a much higher divorce rate and accumulated stress. However, if you love your job and if you (and those close to you) are happy, by all means keep rolling.

Do You Talk Yourself into Failure?

It's human nature to be harder on ourselves than we are on others. But come on, admit it—we all make mistakes. So you're not perfect! Hey,

"Shoot for the moon. Even if you miss, you'll land among the stars."
—*Les Brown*

guess what—you're not the only one. Do you treat yourself with the same compassion and tolerance you offer others, or do you scold yourself for your mistakes, even the small ones?

It may be time to readjust your mindset and cut yourself some slack. If you don't believe in yourself, who will? The more you doubt yourself and mutter under your breath about what you could/should/would do differently, the more you'll talk yourself into believing you're a failure. And really, the only way we truly fail is when we fail to believe in ourselves.

everybody makes mistakes

We are all perfectly capable of making mistakes; in fact, some of us have elevated mistakes to a true art form. But take an optimistic perspective: Mistakes can turn out to be a stroke of luck. Did you know that the discovery of penicillin was a fluke? In 1928, scientist Alexander Fleming was studying a bacteria sample when he spotted something that looked like mold. The mold turned out to be one of the most serendipitous "mistakes" of the century: That mold was penicillin. (Are you an optimist? Flip to page 164 to find out.)

Most of us are not consciously aware of our inner "self-talk," but it profoundly influences our beliefs about ourselves, others, and the world around us. Studies affirm what we already knew: that a hopeful mindset sets your stage for success. It is as easy as dreaming.

Do You Talk Yourself into Failure?

How nice are you—to you?

In the following scenarios, which option more closely matches the way you are likely to think?

1. Your friend Nancy asks you to dog-sit Killer, her crazed pit bull, for a week. You tell yourself:

   a. Last time Nancy brought Killer to my house, he terrorized my cat, had an accident in the family room, shredded the couch pillows, and gnawed on my favorite shoes. But maybe this time won't be so bad.

   b. Keeping Killer would imperil my cat, my carpet, my couch, and my Crocs—and perhaps drive me crazy. I'm sure Nancy will understand when I say no.

2. You meet an attractive new guy or gal. You think to yourself:

   a. Oooh…cute, but waaaay out of my league. This reminds me of that crush I had in high school who could never remember my name.

   b. Hmmmm, cute. How do I look? This could be the beginning....

3. You know your coworkers are going to lunch at La Bella, but no one has mentioned it to you. You think to yourself:

   a. Why don't they want to include me? Is someone mad at me?

   b. I must have missed their call while I was still in that meeting with the head honchos. I'll get my coat!

4. You just learned that you have been chosen to attend a conference in France. You think:

   a. Cripes! I'm not prepared for this! I don't even speak French.

   b. Mon dieu! This is so exciting! I knew my hard work wouldn't go unnoticed.

Do You Talk Yourself into Failure?

5. You decide to duck into a cute little coffee shop for a bagel and espresso. You notice the smartly dressed customers. You think to yourself:

a. I'm underdressed. Compared to all these people, I look like I shop at Goodwill.

b. What a cool little place! This might be an awesome place to meet people. (And those giant oatmeal-raisin cookies look delicious!)

6. You must take an ability test to qualify for a promotion. You think to yourself:

a. What if I don't pass? Everyone will know I failed!

b. Piece of cake! I have what it takes to ace this test.

7. Your date shows up late for the third time in a row, apologizing and explaining there was a can't-miss deadline at work...again. You tell yourself:

a. I should be honest about how much this upsets me, but this is the busy season at work. I don't want to seem unsupportive.

b. I deserve better than this. We need to have a talk.

8. You're trying on jeans in a cool new boutique. You think to yourself:

a. When did I get so fat!? Oh my gosh, my bottom looks huge.

b. These curves are sexy. Should I buy more than one pair?

9. You're reading a research study about the relationship between positive self-talk and increased self-esteem. You think:

a. Yeah, right. I don't believe this bunk. It won't work.

b. I can make my sunny disposition even brighter? Let's give this self-talk stuff a try!

10. You just returned from your physician's office, where you had your annual physical. Your blood pressure is a tad high. You tell yourself:

a. I should have been running or lifting weights. I haven't been eating right, either. What was I thinking?

b. I'll start working on the diet and exercises Dr. D suggested. I'll soon be healthier and in better shape than ever.

Do You Talk Yourself into Failure?

Scoring

Give yourself **1 point** for each "b" answer.

0–3 points
Doubting

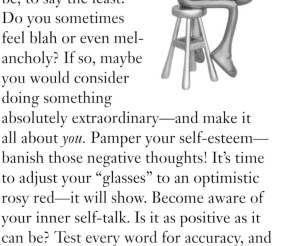

You are not as kind to yourself as you could be, to say the least. Do you sometimes feel blah or even melancholy? If so, maybe you would consider doing something absolutely extraordinary—and make it all about *you*. Pamper your self-esteem—banish those negative thoughts! It's time to adjust your "glasses" to an optimistic rosy red—it will show. Become aware of your inner self-talk. Is it as positive as it can be? Test every word for accuracy, and follow the lead of those detective shows on TV—no matter how attached you are to a theory, if there is no evidence to support it, toss it out.

Try this: Ask ten friends to list several of your most extraordinary characteristics. Now, grab one of those big magnets (pizza delivery–size) off your fridge and post your "extraordinary characteristics" list in a place where you can refer to it often. And don't think you don't deserve the praise!

4–7 points
Getting There

You fit nicely in the middle. You are not especially negative, but your name's not quite Pollyanna, either. If you consider yourself merely okay, however, it's quite possible that you're much better than okay—magnificent, even. Make a conscious choice to be happy and healthy—you're more than halfway there. The more generous and caring you are to yourself, the more positive thoughts you'll have to share with those around you.

8–10 points
Believing

Congratulations! You consistently appreciate who you are, and you've figured out the recipe for success. You are optimistic in many areas of your life, and you know that the more optimistic you are, the greater your chances for success. You don't hold yourself back: Far from talking yourself into failure, you're able to talk yourself into succeeding. The possibilities are limitless—because you believe it.

Do You Put the "Pro" in Procrastinator?

Almost everyone procrastinates at one time or another—either to avoid a mundane task they really don't want to do or to postpone the start of an overwhelming project. Some people are procrastinating pros, happy to postpone virtually any boring or burdensome chore.

> **"Procrastination is something best put off until tomorrow."**
>
> —*Gerald Vaughan*

People procrastinate for many reasons. Some of the most common are lack of motivation, the drive for perfectionism, impulsiveness, and fear. If a person is not motivated, even the smallest task may seem as daunting as trudging up a precipitous slope in a blinding blizzard. Perfectionists want to be...well, perfect...so they may avoid tasks because they don't want to risk failure. Impulsivity is different. Impulsive people tend to throw themselves into something new and exciting and ignore the current task. Fear—of failure, of the unknown—threatens self-confidence and optimism and makes people afraid to try. Whatever the precipitating factor—lack of motivation, perfectionism, impulsiveness, or fear—the job doesn't get done.

Most procrastinators become motivated to change when the pesky habit begins to really drag them down—affecting their life so adversely that it becomes almost impossible for them to succeed. They are willing to take steps to try to change...tomorrow.

Do You Put the "Pro" in Procrastinator?

I never finish anyth...

1. Are you a daydreamer who likes to dream up wonderful, innovative ideas—but doesn't get around to actually creating any of them?

   Yes   No

2. Are you a risk taker who lives for that sweet rush of adrenaline?

   Yes   No

3. Are you comfortable moving beyond your established comfort zone?

   Yes   No

4. Are you so concerned with small details that a project gets lost in the confusion?

   Yes   No

5. Do you end up feeling stressed and bedraggled because you wait until the 11th hour to meet a deadline, and then rush around trying to beat the clock?

   Yes   No

6. Are you confident in your ability to successfully complete projects?

   Yes   No

7. Have you been told that you take on too many tasks?

   Yes   No

8. Do you use avoidance ("if I pretend problems aren't there, they will go away") to "resolve" problems?

   Yes   No

9. When you start on an exciting new project full steam ahead, does your enthusiasm carry through to the end?

   Yes   No

10. When you are in a crunch situation and must hustle to rescue a project, do you feel a rush of adrenaline?

    Yes   No

Do You Put the "Pro" in Procrastinator?

Scoring

Give yourself **1 point** for each time you answered "yes"—except for questions 3, 6, and 9. Give yourself **1 point** for each "no" to 3, 6, and 9. (Hey, all you 8–10 point-ers: Stop dragging your heels. Do it now!)

0–4 points
Hit the Ground Running

You keep procrastination to such a low level that you are probably able to handle almost anything without much loss of productivity. You are organized and efficient, and people know they can rely on you to get a job done.

5–7 points
Stop and Go

So you procrastinate occasionally—who doesn't, right? Perhaps you are taking the time to enjoy your life and loved ones. That's a good thing. As long as you're getting things done without missing too many deadlines or letting anyone down, the effect of your procrastination is probably minimal. Life is a balancing act, and you'll know when you're tipping over.

8–10 points
Dragging Your Heels

If you were really a world-class procrastinator you would not have taken this quiz—until tomorrow. Putting off the unpleasant chores in life isn't a crime; however, it may make your life more stressful. Try making a list of the things you need to do each day—and stick to the list, crossing off each task as you complete it. At the end of the day you'll see concrete evidence of your productivity! If you feel you need some muscle behind you to get you going in the beginning, ask a friend or a coworker to offer assistance and encouragement until "highly productive" becomes a habit for you.

wait for it...

Up to 75 percent of college students freely admit that they are closet procrastinators.

Do You Put the "Pro" in Procrastinator?

what kind of procrastinator are you?

Refer to the quiz questions to help identify the type of procrastinator you are—if you are one at all.

Adrenalin Junkies

Did you answer "yes" to questions 2 and 10? These questions point to an avoider who enjoys the rush only a challenge can provide. You may be a cowboy type who lives for the thrill, or you may even be described as a risk taker. Why not turn to page 136 and take the Are You a Risk Taker quiz?

Intuitive-Idea Folks

Affirmative answers to questions 1 and 8 indicate that you are an intuitive type, or idea person, but are not so good with the follow-through. You may need an organized helper at work and/or at home to help you see your ideas through. For more on intuitive types, check out the Are You Intuitive quiz on page 36.

Unsure Individuals

Do questions 3 and 6 describe your personality? You may be unsure of your ability to handle life's fastballs. Powerful self-confidence is built one success at a time. Begin with small, easy-to-accomplish tasks and work your way up. The Self-Confidence quiz on page 160 addresses this topic more specifically.

Are You Competitive?

Do you take competition seriously? Does your pulse race and your heart pound when you are in the throes of a must-win situation? Though many of us believe, philosophically speaking, that the meek shall inherit the earth, we don't want to play for the meek team. It's our nature to want to be associated with a winning team. For some people, the will to win goes deeper; it's a burning force that drives their daily life. If winning becomes an obsession, there will be a price tag. And the cost can be quite high, such as poor relationships, loneliness, and ruined health.

"A quitter never wins and a winner never quits."
—*Napolean Hill*

Are you the cheerleader who encourages, or are you the win-at-all-costs player who slams all opponents?

survival of the fittest

Some amount of competition makes the world go 'round. Our early ancestors probably competed for the best cave, strongest mate, and biggest beast for dinner. Without this very human need to excel, we might still be living in those primitive caves.

Are You Competitive?

on the flip side

"I wouldn't ever go out and hurt anybody deliberately unless it was, you know, important. Like a league game or something."—Dick Butkus

"Winning isn't everything, but the will to win is everything."—Vince Lombardi

"I never did say that you can't be a nice guy and win. I said that if I was playing third base and my mother rounded third with the winning run, I'd trip her up."
—Leo Durocher

"You've got to get to the stage in life where going for it is more important than winning or losing."
—Arthur Ashe

"Whoever said, 'It's not whether you win or lose that counts,' probably lost."—Martina Navratilova

"Sometimes by losing a battle you find a new way to win the war."
—Donald Trump

"If winning isn't everything, why do they keep score?"—Vince Lombardi

"Ever notice that people never say, 'It's only a game,' when they're winning?"—Ivern Ball

"Losing is no disgrace if you've given your best."—Jim Palmer

"Show me a good loser and I'll show you an idiot."—Leo Durocher

"Winning isn't everything, but losing is nothing."—Red Symons

"A champion needs a motivation above and beyond winning."—Pat Riley

Are You Competitive?

Is winning what it's all about?

1. You and a coworker decide to slim down and tone up. She runs faster than you and doesn't have to stop as often. You think, "I can't let her beat me. I have to push harder."

   True   False

2. In an office meeting your boss praises Ed, a coworker, for work "beyond the call of duty." You think:

   a. What a manipulative, self-serving you-know-what. I do most of the work!

   b. I'm going to have to pull out all of the stops to outshine Ed.

   c. I'm glad Ed is getting some well-deserved attention.

3. There's nothing wrong with the word *overachiever*. Why settle for less?

   True   False

4. You usually drive at least a few miles per hour faster than the speed limit.

   True   False

5. When you were in school, grades were more than just numbers to you; they reflected your worth.

   True   False

6. Your friends invite you to play Monopoly. You think:

   a. No way. I hate losing.

   b. Ooohhh, yeah, time to crush the competition.

   c. Cool, I used to love Monopoly when I was a kid. Should be fun!

7. Every time you watch *The Godfather* you are more impressed by the Corleones' ability to "achieve" against virtually impossible odds.

   True   False

8. There's no such thing as too much competition—at work, in love, or at home.

   True   False

9. You would rather stand out as different when you are in a group of people than keep quiet and agree with the majority.

   True   False

10. Donald Trump is entirely correct: Only the ruthless will survive in the business world.

    True   False

Are You Competitive?

Scoring

Give yourself **1 point** for each time you answered "true." For questions 2 and 6, give yourself **3 points** for "a," **2 points** for "b," and **1 point** for "c." The more points you scored, the more competitive your personality. Rack 'em up, baby!

2–5 points
Laid-back Is the Name of Your Game

You tend to be quiet and contemplative, perhaps an intellectual who seeks learning for its own sake, not for the glory. Winning is icing on the cake for you; you're just happy you can make a contribution to the team. You are self-confident and content to watch the action from the sidelines, and when you do get in the game you're certainly not going to break any rules. You don't feel the need to prove anything to anyone.

6–10 points
Winning Isn't Everything, but It's Something

You enjoy a healthy dash of competition, but you are not fueled by it. Your satisfaction comes from other areas, perhaps: service, humanitarian efforts, or academia. You can hold your own with your peers, but you simply do not live for the finish line. When you win, you acknowledge others' efforts and give them the credit they deserve. You may not feel the need to go for broke every time, but no one should count you out of the game.

11–15 points
Game On!

You bring your "A" game 110 percent of the time, and you genuinely relish the thrill of the chase. Your career probably offers satisfying opportunities for you to achieve and to do battle, such as criminal law, sports, finance, or business. You want to lead the pack and win the gold, and you'll play your heart out to find a way to come out on top.

Are You a Good Coworker?

Do you help your coworkers up the ladder of success, or do you saw off the rungs behind you? We spend many of our waking hours with our coworkers, and if we don't respect each other and connect at an emotional level, those hours can be exceptionally long and tense.

Being a good team player is no more difficult than being a good son or daughter, sibling, spouse, parent, or friend—in fact, it can be considerably less challenging. Yet just about everyone has a work-related horror story or two—or many—to share.

We've all had coworkers that seem to have risen straight from Hades. They disrupt an otherwise cohesive, smoothly running group and make going to work only slightly more appetizing than taking a large dose of castor oil. Some coworkers appear to purposely bug everyone; others

> **If you don't know what to do with many of the papers piled on your desk, stick a dozen colleagues' initials on them and pass them along. When in doubt, route.**
>
> —*Malcolm Forbes*

are annoying, yet don't seem to have a clue. "Annoying" is tolerable if someone is a good team player and a considerate officemate. When neither of these labels apply, however—watch out.

Are You a Good Coworker?

are you a miracle worker?

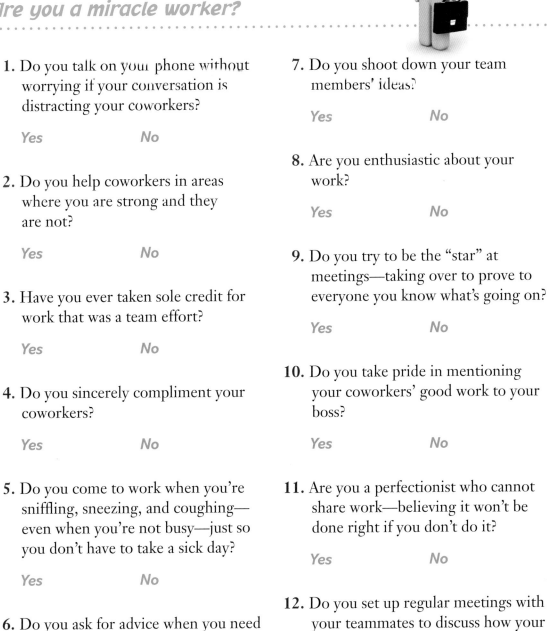

1. Do you talk on your phone without worrying if your conversation is distracting your coworkers?

   Yes   No

2. Do you help coworkers in areas where you are strong and they are not?

   Yes   No

3. Have you ever taken sole credit for work that was a team effort?

   Yes   No

4. Do you sincerely compliment your coworkers?

   Yes   No

5. Do you come to work when you're sniffling, sneezing, and coughing—even when you're not busy—just so you don't have to take a sick day?

   Yes   No

6. Do you ask for advice when you need help?

   Yes   No

7. Do you shoot down your team members' ideas?

   Yes   No

8. Are you enthusiastic about your work?

   Yes   No

9. Do you try to be the "star" at meetings—taking over to prove to everyone you know what's going on?

   Yes   No

10. Do you take pride in mentioning your coworkers' good work to your boss?

    Yes   No

11. Are you a perfectionist who cannot share work—believing it won't be done right if you don't do it?

    Yes   No

12. Do you set up regular meetings with your teammates to discuss how your joint projects are going?

    Yes   No

Are You a Good Coworker?

Scoring

Give yourself **1 point** for each odd-numbered question for which you answered "no"; give yourself **1 point** for each "yes" in the even-numbered questions.

0–3 points
You've Got Your Work
Cut Out for You

It appears that relating well to people at work is not your strength. Perhaps you have noticed that coworkers are chilly toward you at times. While it may be that they are too sensitive, it's more likely that it's time for you to take a long look at your work habits and your behavior at the office. Maybe you're one of the people the rest of the staff would simply rather avoid if possible—but maybe it's worse than that, and your coworkers just don't trust you. To be a better coworker (and to become more popular around the office), watch how your colleagues act and take a cue (and get a clue) from their example.

4–8 points
Working Your Way Up

You're probably not the last person your colleagues would choose to work with, but you're not their first choice, either. You can improve your score considerably by reviewing the questions for which you did not get a point and by asking your coworkers to be totally honest with you. While many of them will try to give you

a nice answer, it's best for you to seek out someone whom you know will be brutally honest—yes, honesty is valuable. Then you will know how to be your best at work. Common sense never hurt, either— if you wouldn't like a behavior in someone else, don't behave that way yourself.

9–12 points
Keep Up the Good Work

You are an excellent, benevolent, and highly regarded coworker. People may be standing in line to work with you and sit near you at the lunch table. Your grammar school teachers taught you well, and you carry the lesson with you: Treat others as you would like to be treated. You are generous in offering help, asking for help (which is a compliment to your peers), and sharing the glory. When you genuinely want to see others succeed, it's likely they'll delight in your success as well. No matter where you work, you will be appreciated.

CHAPTER 5

DO YOU STAND OUT IN A CROWD?

There are people who dance on tables at parties and those who hug the wall. Are you a standout? Do you just naturally turn heads? Maybe you're blessed with animal magnetism, and people are drawn to you like bees to honey.

Are you an enthusiastic, card-carrying party animal? Do you know how to dress to stop traffic? If you do, it can be a great asset. People watch as you go by and wish they could dress with such panache. You may love the spotlight and feel right at home standing center stage in front of a crowd.

Your charisma may separate you from the average person. If people just naturally flock to you and want to be on your team, perhaps you have the irresistible charm of a mega star.

If you are a risk taker, you attract attention without even trying. You simply want to rev up the adrenaline and experience the moment. Go for it!

Do You Have Animal Magnetism?

nimal magnetism is one of the few attributes that cannot be learned: You either have it or you don't. It is feral, instinctive, and very basic. We are all animals, of course, since we don't qualify as vegetables or minerals (regardless of how much of a couch potato you are or how ancient a fossil your mother-in-law might be). However, some of us are more raw, earthier animals than others. Those who have animal magnetism have an innate sense of self-confidence fueled by an inner sense of untamed power, like that of a panther.

Those who have been gifted by nature with animal magnetism have probably noticed that people are inexplicably drawn to them, tend to seek out their company, and follow their lead gratefully, thanks to the sheer magnetism of their personality.

He has that nameless charm, with a strong magnetism, which can only be called 'It.'

—*Elinor Glyn*

If you have an exceptional ability to captivate and influence people with your very presence, perhaps you have what no money can buy: powerful animal magnetism.

Do You Have Animal Magnetism?

are you naturally captivating?

Respond to the following statements by checking the box that most closely matches your personality.

	Slightly like me	Moderately like me	Very much like me
1. I am always dressed and groomed to perfection—appearance is very important.	☐	☐	☐
2. I am a good storyteller; I use body language, wit, and emotion.	☐	☐	☐
3. Some people describe me as a rebel, dancing to the beat of a different drummer.	☐	☐	☐
4. I am the Rembrandt of my career.	☐	☐	☐
5. I have received the winning popular vote to an office or position at work or school.	☐	☐	☐
6. My presence overcomes the rough waters and smoothes the ruffled tail feathers in any group.	☐	☐	☐
7. It's normal for several members of the opposite sex to be vying for my attention at the same time.	☐	☐	☐
8. Everyone furtively checks me out when I enter a room.	☐	☐	☐

Do You Have Animal Magnetism?

	Slightly like me	Moderately like me	Very much like me
9. When I talk, others hang on my every word.	☐	☐	☐
10. Coworkers and friends want to be on my side of an issue.	☐	☐	☐

Scoring

Give yourself **1 point** for "Slightly like me," **2 points** for "Moderately like me," and **3 points** for "Very much like me."

10–15 points
Wise Owl

We all have some magnetism, but perhaps your gifts lie in another direction. Maybe you are a more cognitive or intuitive person who leads with your head or your emotions—these are certainly traits that keep you headed in the right direction.

16–25 points
Proud Peacock

Without a doubt, you have some animal magnetism. You are self-confident, a natural leader, and a powerful presence. You are focused and cunning, and you have the tenacity to achieve your goals.

26–30 points
Soaring Falcon

You have that enchanting glow of animal magnetism that people are powerless to resist. No doubt you're a very effective communicator, you present yourself well, and are successful in your career. It's likely you have many admirers and are quite popular. Others may perceive an edge to your personality.

Are You a Party Animal?

Most of us love a good party. However, "good party" is a relative term—it could mean *"rock out until 6:00 A.M. and hope the police can't find the address"* or *"enjoy a spot of tea and cookies in the garden."* What kind of shindig do you enjoy?

While a true party animal may live to whoop it up at the loudest, longest, and wildest bash, plenty of other people know how to have fun too. As long as you have a good time, you can consider the get-together a success. So whether your next party invitation requires a formal RSVP or a knock at the door and a secret password, you know it's time to clear your calendar and get ready to have a ball.

> **"Nothing makes you more tolerant of a neighbor's noisy party than being there."**
>
> —*Franklin P. Jones*

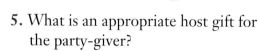

Are You a Party Animal?

are you ready to party hearty?

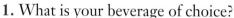
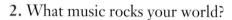

1. What is your beverage of choice?
   a. A glass of Chardonnay
   b. A Mai Tai or two
   c. "What's My Name Again?" shooters—and keep 'em coming

2. What music rocks your world?
   a. Barry Manilow
   b. U2
   c. Metallica

3. What is the shutdown time for party animals?
   a. After the local evening news
   b. It depends on how much fun you're having
   c. After the cock crows

4. What would you wear to feel your hottest and most attractive?
   a. Whatever you wore to the office that day
   b. Something trendy and flattering
   c. Something outrageous that makes you look as good as you feel (but not so tight you can't get your dancing groove on!)

5. What is an appropriate host gift for the party-giver?
   a. *The Joy of Cooking*
   b. An iTunes gift card
   c. 80-proof anything

6. What are acceptable party games?
   a. Charades, bridge, and backgammon
   b. Pictionary, Loaded Questions, and Scattergories
   c. Beer Bungee, Truth or Dare, and Pennies in a Pitcher

7. Who should you take with you to a party?
   a. Your sister, who's training to be a police officer
   b. Your roommate or significant other
   c. Everyone who wants to come!

8. What constitutes appropriate small talk?
   a. The economy
   b. This season's *American Idol* finalists
   c. How crazy everyone got at last night's party

122

Are You a Party Animal?

9. What time do you get out of the bed the morning after a good party?

   a. 8:00 A.M. (8:30 or 9:00 if it was a *really* good party)

   b. When the sunlight finally wakes you

   c. *Morning?* Yeah, right.

10. What's your favorite type of gathering?

   a. A Tupperware party

   b. A Super Bowl party

   c. A rave

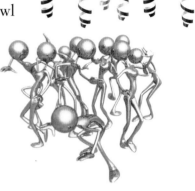

Scoring

More "a" answers
Sedate

The good news is you're not out of control. The bad news is you probably will not be receiving many invitations to wild parties—or maybe you consider that *good* news. You are far too civilized to qualify as a party animal.

More "b" answers
Fun-Loving

You know how to have a fun night out, but sometimes you'd choose a night in with your pals, chitchatting, playing board games, and enjoying some snacks and beverages. You enjoy a good party, but you're not going to quit your day job.

More "c" answers
Wild and Crazy

Ah, now we get down to the genuine article. Hello, party animal! Are you just waking up from your crazy night out? You live for the next party, and that's okay, but you may want to take a night off every now and then and give yourself a rest.

Do You Dress to Kill?

Many studies, and our own common sense and experience, tell us that appearance is important. It can be particularly important when meeting someone for the first time. The cliché is true: You never get a second chance to make a first impression.

Each of us has our own personal style of dressing and grooming. Much depends on our personalities and how we see ourselves. Some people have elevated "dress to kill" to an art form; for others, jeans and a T-shirt may suffice. Of course, our profession impacts our clothing choices (the casual approach probably won't work for a stockbroker or an attorney); however, personality chooses profession. Everything is connected!

> **"Why not be oneself? That is the whole secret of a successful appearance. If one is a greyhound, why try to look like a Pekingese?"**
>
> —Dame Edith Sitwell

Do You Dress to Kill?

What's your sense of style?

For each question, choose the answer that suits you to a "T."

1. Which best describes your wardrobe?

   a. At least a couple of power suits

   b. Jeans and T-shirts

   c. Button-down shirts; skirts and slacks in clean, classic lines

   d. Brightly colored tops and dresses that fit like a glove

   e. Stylish, trendy, very now

2. Which colors do you gravitate to?

   a. Navy, charcoal, and black—and sometimes cream

   b. Faded denim and indigo

   c. Crisp white, khaki, and blue—plus the occasional forest green

   d. Red, black, sparkles—whatever catches my eye (and yours)

   e. Black, ivory, or whatever I see in the pages of this month's *Vogue*

3. Which best describes your closet?

   a. Color-coordinated—like colors together, graduating light to dark

   b. A few items hanging—most folded and placed on the shelves

   c. Organized but not compulsive—pants on one side, shirts on the other

   d. A jumble of bright colors—shade your eyes!

   e. A revolving door of couture—price tags still on the newest items

4. Which of the following laundering choices appeals to you?

   a. I bring everything to the dry cleaner for professional handling and a crisp crease

   b. Into the washer, out of the dryer: Done

   c. Whatever the tags advise

   d. Much of my wardrobe is hand-wash only

   e. If I don't wear something more than once, I don't have to clean it

5. Which best describes your look?

   a. Upscale and professional

   b. Comfortable

   c. Wrinkle-free and high-quality

   d. Expensive, soft, stretchy, touchable

   e. Whatever slinks down the runway

Do You Dress to Kill?

Scoring

More "a" answers
Powerful and Proud

You are aggressive, a winner, and you dress the part. Your profession is competitive, and the stakes are high. You know that you must do everything possible to gain an edge, and your attire makes a powerful statement about your ability, confidence, and commitment. No doubt you are moving up the ladder and loving the challenge.

More "b" answers
Laid-back and Low-key

You are quietly confident; there is neither pretense nor need for show in your low-key style. You value comfort, and nothing is more comfortable than jeans—old, well-worn jeans, definitely not the $200 variety sold today. Your profession is likely to be hassle-free artsy, academic, or humanitarian. Keep grooving along, enjoying the adventure.

More "c" answers
Traditional

Your conservative clothes look nice but don't draw a lot of attention. It's likely you value family, your commitments, and tradition. You are comfortable with procedure, plans, and appropriate rules, and it's likely

you've chosen a structured career such as teaching, accounting, medicine, or law. That doesn't mean that you don't enjoy a healthy dose of fun—you've even been known to be the life of the party. Bottom line: You see no need for pretentiousness, whether designer, power tie, or patently "casual."

More "d" answers
Sensual and Fun

You are self-confident and sensual and not afraid to show it. You have class nicely mixed with charming allure, and you dress to look your best and let your personality shine through. You may be quite successful in your profession—do you work in the arts? Maybe you're a recording artist, painter, writer, dancer, actress, or art teacher. Whatever your field, you are bold and unique, with a strong sense of style and the self-confidence that comes naturally with self-awareness.

More "e" answers
Chic and Daring

You are not a wallflower. Wherever you go (the best restaurants, the hottest parties, the trendiest coffee bars), you want to stand out. You don't just follow the trends: You carry the fashion banner.

Do You Dress to Kill?

Your friends know if they follow your lead, they won't look like last year's model. It's likely your occupation is something that requires dare and flair. You fit in especially well in sales (e.g. real estate, high-end automobiles, or jewelry), fashion design or consulting, media, or politics. You are admired and emulated.

Combination of all five
Eclectic

You are a wild card who doesn't fall easily into just one category. You do your own thing depending on your mood. Your career path? Whatever you want it to be!

spinning the color wheel

Black is powerful, chic, and always in style. Remember the classic battle of black versus white, and you'll know that black usually carries an air of danger.

White is clean, pure, innocent, or open. Pure as the driven snow, anyone?

Red is energetic, motivating, bold, powerful, or outrageous. Red is also the traditional color of love and romance.

Blue can be peaceful and tranquil, or it can be electric and shocking. Blue is a regal color and the cool color of ice (and diamonds). Many people list blue as their favorite color.

Today, **green** means responsible: eco-friendly and doing our part to save the planet. Green is also associated with Ireland, wealth, and nature. Green is a cool and relaxing color.

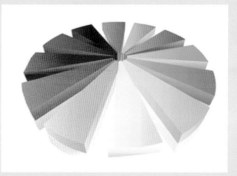

Orange is full of energy—warm, bold, and exciting.

Pink is often associated with women and girls, though men are beginning to test the waters with shades both bright and pale. On them, pink can be fresh and daring; historically, pink is a very Victorian, romantic color.

Yellow is sunny and bright and can be startlingly bold. Pale buttercup yellow is relaxing; bold yellow is energizing. Yellow is said to help with concentration.

Are You a Spotlight-Seeker?

"All the world's a stage."

—*William Shakespeare*

We all enjoy a little attention from the significant people in our lives, and some of us enjoy a lot of attention—from everyone. Everyone knows someone who is a natural "star"—who's exceptionally adept at standing center stage and celebrating the moment in a brilliant beam of Hollywood sunshine, while others prefer to stand backstage and maneuver the curtain.

Homecoming queens, class clowns, pop singers, and television news anchors habitually seek out and capture the limelight. Others who may not be comfortable center stage find themselves thrust there anyway—perhaps because of their special talents (think Albert Einstein) or their affiliation with spotlight-seekers (think Laura Bush). Even if they don't choose fame and even if they don't particularly enjoy it, they simply can't avoid being shoved forward.

Do you frequently find yourself at the center of attention? And if so, do you enjoy the experience, or would you rather fade into the background?

Are You a Spotlight-Seeker?

Do you want the lead role, or would you prefer a backstage pass?

Which sentiment most closely describes your feelings?

	Hello! This is so me!	I'll think about it.	Ooohh, I don't think so.
1. The local theater is asking wannabe stars to try out for their production of *My Fair Lady*. I'm first in line to try out for the lead.	❏	❏	❏
2. My life philosophy leans toward functional rather than playful and exuberant.	❏	❏	❏
3. My supervisor is urging us to practice our public speaking skills. I suggest a high-tech, high-profile presentation for the higher-ups—by me.	❏	❏	❏
4. If I could redo one room in my home, I would add a leather recliner, fill the walls with books, and turn it into my very own warm, inviting library.	❏	❏	❏

Are You a Spotlight-Seeker?

	Hello! This is so me!	I'll think about it.	Ooohh, I don't think so.
5. Recently my friends and I went to a party that turned slightly *Animal House.* Grooving to the deafening din, I ran to the stage and grabbed a mic to sing along with the band.	❏	❏	❏
6. When I am out with a bunch of my buds, I love to sit back, chill, and enjoy their funny stories.	❏	❏	❏
7. My ideal car is an eye-catching coupe with sleek, sexy curves. Even better: Make that a convertible.	❏	❏	❏
8. Though I thoroughly enjoy outings with my friends, sometimes I prefer to stay in and unwind.	❏	❏	❏
9. I love to dress in vibrant colors such as tomato red, dazzling blue, and luminous yellow.	❏	❏	❏
10. My career requires me to teach, speak, and/or mingle with diverse groups, and I'm often over-whelmed by the interaction.	❏	❏	❏

Are You a Spotlight-Seeker?

Scoring

For all odd-numbered statements, please give yourself **3 points** for "Hello! This is so me!," **2 points** for "I'll think about it," and **1 point** for "Ooohh, I don't think so." Reverse that for the even-numbered statements, giving yourself **3 points** for "Ooohh, I don't think so," **2** for "I'll think about it," and **1** for " Hello! This is so me!"

10–15 points
Behind the Scenes

You are probably slightly introverted, perhaps intellectual, and you enjoy the warm comfort of the background. You do not feel pressured to prove yourself, and the spotlight holds no allure. You enjoy people, but you are perfectly happy backstage during the performance. Your presence is felt and valued, yet you do little to actively encourage attention. Maybe, just maybe, you'll come out from backstage to pass out programs or usher people to their seats.

16–25 points
Somewhere in Between

You like to strut your stuff at times and you enjoy basking in appreciation, yet it is not a significant motivating factor in your life. Part of the cast, stagehand, PR manager—you're happy to fill whichever role you're needed in. Perhaps you're one of those people of exceptional talent who are thrust into the limelight. You've learned to handle that with grace and good humor, but it was not your first choice. You do what is necessary and will play your part quite well, yet you do not aggressively seek the limelight.

25–30 points
Queen of the Silver Screen

All the world's a stage—and you are the star. You are definitely a center-stage person, and you glow with an inner luminosity when the big lights focus on you. You don't need a great deal of preparation for a starring role in life; you are naturally effervescent. When you step to the podium to accept your Oscar, be sure to remember to thank the little people who helped you get where you are today. Lights, camera, roll 'em....

Are You Charismatic?

Consider Oprah Winfrey, Barack Obama, George Clooney, Tom Cruise. What do they have in common? They radiate charisma—a luminous charm that draws people to them and makes us feel special. Though we may have some difficulty defining charisma, most of us recognize it when it stands in front of us. You know immediately if someone is simply oozing charm and self-confidence...and so does every other person in the room.

What is the secret of charisma? Is it that charismatic people are happy and make others feel happy? It's obvious that happy individuals like themselves, and they may appear to sparkle with the sheer marvel and delight of being. This inner glow and supreme self-assurance is irresistible.

> **The reason we're successful, darling? My overall charisma, of course.**
>
> *—Freddie Mercury*

charisma is not always a good thing

Some people will flaunt a "false" charisma, passing it off as stunning self-confidence. For instance, people in the "popular" crowd may be extraordinarily charming and beguilingly fluent, and can attract people like flies. You may be drawn in by this type of manipulator. Please take our quiz on "givers and takers" (page 46) to determine if you are susceptible to these charming takers.

The benefits of charisma cannot be overestimated: It can attract romantic partners, elicit enough attention to catapult you to the next rung of the career ladder—even help you garner enough votes to win a seat in public office. Charisma is evidenced, in part, by gutsy risk-taking and a cool self-confidence. (Lucky for you we have a quiz on both! See pages 136 and 160.)

Are You Charismatic?

How charismatic are you?

Mark the degree to which you agree or disagree with the following statements.

	Strongly disagree	Disagree	Agree	Strongly agree
1. I am fortunate to have many close, devoted friends.	❏	❏	❏	❏
2. Somehow, I always seem to find myself the center of attention.	❏	❏	❏	❏
3. People enjoy my witty sense of humor.	❏	❏	❏	❏
4. Adventure appeals to me.	❏	❏	❏	❏
5. My success is a foregone conclusion.	❏	❏	❏	❏
6. Friends and coworkers seek my advice.	❏	❏	❏	❏
7. Conquering new circumstances is easy for me.	❏	❏	❏	❏
8. People generally listen attentively when I speak.	❏	❏	❏	❏

ADVENTUROUS

CENTER OF ATTENTION

Are You Charismatic?

	Strongly disagree	Disagree	Agree	Strongly agree
9. I am energized by public speaking.	☐	☐	☐	☐
10. I am always myself in social situations; I don't pretend to be someone I'm not.	☐	☐	☐	☐
11. People tell me I make them feel good.	☐	☐	☐	☐
12. Sincere praise is liberally sprinkled in my conversations with others.	☐	☐	☐	☐
13. I am at my charming best when I meet new people.	☐	☐	☐	☐
14. I am energetic and passionate about my work.	☐	☐	☐	☐
15. I am genuinely warm and caring.	☐	☐	☐	☐

CARING

ENERGETIC

Are You Charismatic?

Scoring

Give yourself **0 points** for each "Strongly disagree," **1 point** for "Disagree," **2 points** for "Agree," and **3 points** for "Strongly agree."

0–20 points
A Bit Anemic

Have you been a bit harsh in your judgments? Self-assurance is the foundation of charisma. Perhaps you should examine your negative beliefs about yourself with someone you trust—someone who is optimistic. Confidence can be learned one positive experience at a time, and self-confidence is at the root of charisma. Positive experiences are sometimes open to interpretation—please be generous when interpreting. Your charisma quotient can grow by leaps and bounds. Now, go out there and dazzle!

21–35 points
A Healthy Dose

You are aware of your many personal strengths. You are doing well, you probably have close and meaningful relationships, and your life is quite... comfortable. Do you yearn to pass comfortable and go straight to fabulous, thrilling, and phenomenal? Charisma can be intensified. It can hit the stratosphere, and you can do it. Listen to your thoughts: Question negative beliefs, and know that your thoughts are not necessarily reality—they are merely your perception of reality. The more confidence you have in yourself, the more charisma you will radiate.

36–45 points
Daily Requirement Reached

Your charisma is obvious for all to see. You enjoy excelling. You are dizzy with excitement about life and your future. The people in your life adore you, and you genuinely appreciate them. Your career excites you, and you head to work each day envisioning the electrifying possibilities. Every phone call and e-mail is a potential adventure filled with drama and promise. Your priorities are well drawn, and there is no end in sight.

Are You a Risk Taker?

Daredevils go for the gusto in life. They seem to need, and seem to thrive on, more adrenaline than the average population. According to a recent study, risk takers are likely to be in their teens and 20s rather than middle-aged, and they tend to

"If you define cowardice as running away at the first sign of danger, screaming and tripping and begging for mercy, then yes, Mr. Brave man, I guess I'm a coward."
—Jack Handey

be taller than the norm. Daredevils are also aggressively high in testosterone and light on estrogen. It probably doesn't come as a shock to learn that studies show men are more likely to be risk takers than women. However, that seems to be slowly changing as women are gravitating in larger numbers to previously male-dominated hazardous occupations.

Interestingly, people who say they are satisfied with their life are more likely to be risk takers than those who don't report a high level of satisfaction. Bottom line: Statistically speaking, if you are a happy, tall, young male you are probably more willing to jump on a motorcycle or pilot a jet than, say, your older, smaller sister would be. But nothing is out of the question, as this quiz will show you.

ah, the innocence of youth

Although you don't have to be young to be a risk taker, it certainly helps. Research shows that humans' brain circuitry is not fully functional until their early 20s—or even later. This explains a great deal about the enthusiasm of youth, doesn't it?

Are You a Risk Taker?

are you a daredevil or a nervous nellie?

Put a checkmark in the box that best describes your attitude.

	Surely you jest	Sometimes	That's me— Woo-hoo!
1. In my wayward youth, I was always the first one to say, "Don't worry, we won't get caught."	❑	❑	❑
2. If I had lived during Prohibition, I would have built my own still and opened up a speakeasy.	❑	❑	❑
3. I love sexy sports cars with a dangerous edge.	❑	❑	❑
4. I would rather buy a Jet Ski today than a house next year.	❑	❑	❑
5. I always leave a window or a door open in case I feel the urge to roam.	❑	❑	❑
6. I enjoy many and varied romantic adventures.	❑	❑	❑
7. I frequently hear, "Are you crazy? You can't do that!" from friends, family, and coworkers. (They are mistaken.)	❑	❑	❑

Are You a Risk Taker?

	Surely you jest	Sometimes	That's me— Woo-hoo!
8. My motto is "Step aside, I'll go first."	☐	☐	☐
9. I am confident that I am in control no matter what I do.	☐	☐	☐
10. When in a social or business group, I shock some people by speaking boldly (and sometimes recklessly).	☐	☐	☐
11. I am in a high-risk occupation and love every minute of it.	☐	☐	☐
12. I've been offered a great job in a distant city where I don't know a soul. Time to pack my bags, grab the GPS, and hit the road (on my Harley)!	☐	☐	☐

Scoring

Give yourself **1 point** for each "Surely you jest," **2 points** for "Sometimes," and **3 points** for "That's me—Woo-hoo!"

12–20 points
Slow and Steady

You are not thrilled about jumping into danger feet first. You live a more judicious, traditional lifestyle and tend to solemnly consider your decisions before doing anything rash. You probably took a few risks in the past, but they are not your fondest memories. Although your life has not been filled with adventure, you are probably comfortable and on a path to success in your career and relationships. Others know what to expect from you, and they find that comforting. Maybe someday you'll decide to go wild and buy some risky stocks just for the sheer pleasure of the adrenaline rush—and that's okay. Go for it!

Are You a Risk Taker?

21–30 points
Balancing Act

You are inclined to take a risk; however, you study the risk very carefully and leave little to chance.
At times, this has worked quite well for you.

You may have picked up a few financial hints that worked to your advantage, but you also may have been wary of others that could have been disastrous—or could have paid off in huge profits. You consider one risk at a time before choosing the adrenaline rush or the safety valve. The problem is, a risk can go either way, and you never know what the toss of the dice will bring. Taking risks requires practice; it's up to you to decide if you want to play it safe or take a chance.

31–36 points
Living on the Edge

Greetings, daredevil. You totally enjoy playing the game—win or lose. To you, the lure of danger is irresistible. Living on the edge, walking the tightrope, has its exhilarating rewards, and they become addictive. You make the rules by which you live, and you wouldn't have it any other way. (By the way, have you had a serious conversation with your life insurance agent recently? Keep your friends close and your agent closer.)

fun fact

Both men and women are attracted to risk takers—go figure.

CHAPTER 6

WELLNESS

Wellness is maintenance to prevent illness and premature aging. Just as you get regular maintenance for your car to keep it humming, you can be proactive about your health—including your emotional well-being. Stress ages us beyond our years and can compromise our health. How bulked up is your willpower? You may need strong willpower to keep yourself exercising regularly and eating healthfully.

Suspicious people and those who don't cope well aren't as happy or as healthy as optimists and self-confident folks. Do you expect good things to happen? Do you expect the best from others? Then you will probably get exactly those things.

Take these quizzes and learn how to be proactive to stay strong and healthy in mind and spirit. Keep up your maintenance—you'll be glad that you did.

Are You Chilled Out or Stressed Out?

How well do you handle stress? Are you naturally calm, cool, and collected, or does your pulse race fast enough to win the Kentucky Derby? Not all nervous systems are created equal, and personality plays a significant role in how you react to 5:00 traffic jams, bothersome coworkers, and the vicissitudes of the 21st century.

Stress is a nebulous concept. A situation that is acutely stressful to one person may be the equivalent of a broken fingernail to another. Fortunately, we have considerable control over our stress reactions. Are you tired of the stress and ready to fight back?

"Give your stress wings and let it fly away."

—Carin Hartness

If you eat your veggies and wild salmon, drink your green tea, and hit the machines at the gym, your wellness and your ability to handle stress will soar. In addition, studies show that genetics play a large role in how people cope with stress, so if you were wise enough to choose parents with awesome genetics, lucky you! If not, well, you still have steamed cabbage and a treadmill.

Are You Chilled Out or Stressed Out?

How well do you cope with stress?

How well do these statements match your personality? Put a checkmark in the appropriate box.

	No way, dude	Could be	That's me—how did you know?
1. I am not comfortable delegating work, so I usually end up trying to do everything myself. Often, I feel exhausted by the end of the day.	☐	☐	☐
2. I feel as if I am an ER doc moving from one crisis to the next.	☐	☐	☐
3. I have very few close, supportive friends.	☐	☐	☐
4. I find myself getting frustrated and annoyed with sales clerks and servers.	☐	☐	☐
5. I feel anxious if my work is not flawless.	☐	☐	☐
6. I have a task at work—due tomorrow. I panic and move into overdrive, trying to outrun the steadily ticking clock.	☐	☐	☐

Are You Chilled Out or Stressed Out?

	No way, dude	Could be	That's me—how did you know?
7. I have been indulging in comfort foods such as candy bars and French fries more than usual.	❏	❏	❏
8. I often feel like I'm running behind schedule and there's no way to catch up.	❏	❏	❏
9. Procrastination has become a way of life. I put off going to the grocery store until the refrigerator is empty and the cupboard is almost bare.	❏	❏	❏
10. I just found out that my sweetie will be home in half an hour and ready for dinner—with a group of pals. I throw my hands in the air, scream, and run for the border.	❏	❏	❏

Are You Chilled Out or Stressed Out?

Scoring

Give yourself **1 point** for "No way, dude," **2 points** for "Could be," and **3 points** for "That's me—how did you know?"

10–17 points
Chilled Out

You are as laid-back as it gets. Either you have been blessed with rock-solid genes (lucky you!) or you have found the coping skills you need—or both. You don't respond to daily crises with more emotion than they deserve. You have probably learned that nothing is the end of the world (except, of course, the end of the world). Everything else can be handled—no sweat. You are way cool. It wouldn't hurt to keep in mind, however, that in order to succeed in today's society, you must have a spark to light your fire when you need it.

18–25 points
Balancing the Pressure

You have effective coping tools, and you are using them. Your stress symptoms are nominal, and you are probably enjoying a life spread out comfortably among family, friends, and work. You have found a way to balance these roles with only a moderate dose of anxiety. Keeping a slight edge will help you stay sharp and focused; for example, think about taking a test or giving a presentation at work. That slight tinge of anxiety will drive you to prepare for it, but too much anxiety would sabotage your work. This quiz indicates that you have just the right balance to succeed.

26–30 points
Stressed Out

The good news is—you are human. The bad news is, too much stress is not healthy, and you seem to be experiencing a significant amount. It's possible you are simply going through a particularly challenging period in your life. If this is your baseline level, however, you may need to develop a few stress-coping techniques (see "Coping with Stress," opposite page) and work on your wellness with healthful foods and exercise. More great news: Good nutrition and adequate physical activity will do wonders for reducing your stress quotient.

Are You Chilled Out or Stressed Out?

coping with stress

To push your score closer to "Chilled Out," try these strategies:

Try some deep breathing. Breathe in through your nose, hold it for several seconds, and breathe out slowly through your mouth. Do this four or five times, and you'll feel your stress level plummet.

Share your concerns with friends and family. Someone who allows you to vent your emotions and to freely express your thoughts is worth his or her weight in gold.

Keep a journal of your thoughts and feelings. Writing helps you organize your thoughts and release pent-up emotions.

Slow down and remind yourself to keep everything in perspective.

Get plenty of exercise. And at times of extreme stress, go for a run or hit the gym. A good workout will help you blow off some steam.

Eat healthful foods. Good health will help you in all areas of your life!

Is Your Willpower Strong or Struggling?

Willpower is that voice in your head that says, "Stay focused on your goal"—whatever that may be. Maybe you want to lose a few pounds, improve your GPA, watch less TV; a goal is simply anything you want to accomplish. And willpower is the ability to turn your back on temptations that threaten to knock you off track. For example, it takes willpower to say no to the chocolate éclair that's calling your name.

The "pleasure principle" is your willpower's nemesis. It says, "But that éclair looks so delicious... I want it NOW!" It takes determination to remain focused on your long-term goal and not to give in to the siren call of the pleasure principle. Of course, there's no such thing as ironclad when it comes to willpower and, unfortunately, there is no secret formula for obtaining it either.

"Act as if you are and you will become such." —Leo Tolstoy

Do you need to dig deep to find the determination to turn your back on temptation, or are you lucky enough to have an innate ability to stick to your resolve?

Is Your Willpower Strong or Struggling?

Does your willpower need a workout?

Choose the response that best describes what you would do in each situation.

1. It's Christmas Eve, and you find yourself alone for a moment, gazing at the dazzling tree. You notice that one of the beautifully wrapped gifts has your name on it and a piece of tape has come loose. You would:

   a. "Help" the rest of the tape loosen, and take a little peek.

   b. Retape the wrapping paper and not even think about peeking.

   c. Consider the pros and cons of opening the present, decide "no, that wouldn't be fair," and go to bed.

2. You have resolved to eat better and improve your nutrition so you can live to be 100. The next day, you go out to lunch with friends who order cheeseburgers, pizza, and cheesecake. You would:

   a. Go ahead and order the lasagna. Why be a wet blanket?

   b. Order a nice little salad with turkey for protein. Obviously, your friends don't care if they reach 100!

   c. Be sorely tempted by the fatty goodies, but bite the bullet and order a turkey sandwich with a side salad.

3. You set your sights on making the most of that gym membership, and you've been scheduling your workouts every day after work. Today, as you leave the office, you feel a slight headache coming on. You would:

   a. Go home. Working out would probably make this headache worse.

   b. Drive to the gym anyway. Headache or no headache, it is workout time.

   c. Head to the gym and see how it goes. The headache might get worse, but then again, it might get better.

Is Your Willpower Strong or Struggling?

4. You want to get along well with your coworkers. In fact, you'd like to get to know a couple of them better—but you can't decide which one you want to ask out. You would:

   a. Ask them both out—for different nights. No one will know!

   b. Rather not date coworkers; it can lead to problems.

   c. Ask one or two of them if they want to grab a cup of coffee after work—it doesn't hurt to be friendly.

5. Your goal is to respect your partner's privacy, and you expect the same in return. You see his or her cell phone sitting on the desk. You would:

   a. Make certain the coast is clear, then take a tiny look-see at the incoming and outgoing calls.

   b. Do nothing. It's not right to snoop around someone else's phone.

   c. Wonder—casually—who your sweetie was talking to this morning, then go read a book.

6. You need to be at work by 8:00 A.M. Your alarm goes off at 6:30—giving you just enough time to get ready for work and get yourself there on time. But you're so tired! You would:

   a. Push the snooze button and grab a few more Z's—another few minutes won't matter.

   b. Pop out of bed and head for the steaming coffee pot—programmed the night before to be brewed by 6:29 A.M.

   c. Crawl out of bed, wander around in circles for a few minutes—seriously consider falling back into bed—and head groggily toward the shower.

7. You want to stay connected with your mom and dad and know what is going on in their lives. The folks invite you to dinner on Saturday night. You would:

   a. Love to visit them, but going out with the gang on Saturday night will be lots more fun. We'll get together another time.

   b. Be there 30 minutes early—with flowers.

   c. Invite them to dinner another night instead, telling them you have a prior commitment on Saturday.

Is Your Willpower Strong or Struggling?

8. Times are tough, and you have decided to try to put away a little nest egg. You love your $5 gourmet coffee on the way into work every morning, but you realize what a difference that money could make toward building up your savings. You would:

a. Not give up the mocha delights (they're a key component in starting the day off right!) and decide to save in some other area.

b. A penny saved is a penny earned—good-bye, gourmet coffee.

c. Decide to splurge on a mocha latte once or twice a week instead of every day—that saves $15 or $20 a week, and it turns the coffee into a treat to look forward to, as well.

9. You have decided to clean your home and get organized floor to ceiling. It's the weekend, and you have two days to redo your closets. You would:

a. Think about getting started on those closets, but take a little time for some fun first—it's the weekend! The closets will still be there tomorrow.

b. Pop out of bed bright and early and get right to work—it's best to take advantage of the whole day.

c. Sleep a little late, have a nice breakfast, then start sorting the bedroom closet.

10. You want to be a loyal, compassionate friend. Your best friend, Fred, told you he's attracted to Deb, but he isn't ready to tell her yet. When Deb invites you out for lunch, you:

a. Accept, then get carried away and accidentally let slip that Fred has more than friendship on his mind.

b. Immediately make up an excuse to avoid being alone with Deb; it's not smart to take any chances.

c. Go to lunch, and despite wanting to tell her about Fred, resist the urge and talk about plans for the weekend instead.

Is Your Willpower Strong or Struggling?

Scoring

Mostly "a" answers
The Gregarious Free Spirit

You're doing your best with what you have at the moment. Your intentions may be good; unfortunately, you haven't yet become able to consistently follow through on all of your goals. When you do reach your goal, you will feel fabulous about your success—as you should. Demanding more of yourself (which means having confidence in your ability to succeed) will put you over the finish line more often. Trust yourself: You can save money, get healthy, and thrive at work. These are attainable goals—just learn to exercise that willpower consistently!

Mostly "b" answers
The First Sarge

Your willpower is off the scale! You can be proud of your ability to get things done and stick to your guns. But are you taking enough time to do the things you enjoy? You have the willpower thing down pat; now may be the time to decide what you truly take pleasure in and give yourself permission to spend some time doing it. At first, you may feel guilty, but that's okay. Think of it this way: You've just set yourself another goal—to have fun. You can be successful, responsible, and honor-able and still have room for relaxation, entertainment, and silliness—they are not mutually exclusive.

Mostly "c" answers
The Acrobat

You are able to walk with admirable balance between Dionysus and Mother Teresa. You have managed to combine the need to live fully with the desire to grow and thrive. You know that while taking the high road is admirable, at times it is okay to relax the iron will and simply enjoy each precious moment.

A mixture of all three answers
Ambivalent and Learning

You don't neatly fall into any category—not even the middle. You take things as they come and have more willpower at some times than at others. Perhaps you are working on being more consistent, or maybe you are satisfied with the way you handle challenges. Goals and gutsy will-power tip our lives toward structure and achievement. Maybe you want to consider exercising your willpower and bulking up those resolve muscles. It can pay off in a more predictable future—not always a bad thing.

Suspicious Mind?
Why Do You Ask?

Why can't you see what you are doing to me?
We can't go on together with suspicious minds.
And we can't build our dreams on suspicious minds.

—Elvis Presley

Read the lyrics. You don't even have to read between the lines to see that there are some serious trust issues at work here. Are you a suspicious person, too? Do you generally boast thoughts of goodwill and have faith in your friends and acquaintances, or are you more comfortable admitting nothing, denying everything, and demanding photographs? While a healthy smidgeon of suspicion can be a very good thing, not so if we take wariness to extremes and expect everyone to have Machiavellian intent.

> **"We can gain no lasting peace if we approach it with suspicion and mistrust or with fear."**
>
> —*Franklin D. Roosevelt*

Do you seek the best in people, as even Darth Vader did, when he lamented, "I find your lack of faith disturbing"? Or does the title of Al Franken's book, *Lies and the Lying Liars Who Tell Them*, pretty much sum up your thoughts?

Suspicious Mind? Why Do You Ask?

Judicious or suspicious?

For each question, choose the option that most closely represents your philosophy.

1. You are in the market for a slightly used car. You take one look at the used-car sales representative and think:

   a. He or she is out here trying to make a living.

   b. Hmmmm, I've heard some stories about the trustworthiness (or lack thereof) of used-car salespeople—I'll remain watchful.

   c. If I don't believe a word they say, I may survive.

2. Your spoiled younger brother, Diamond Jim, says he wants to borrow $5,000 to start an after-school program for disadvantaged youth in his neighborhood. In all the time you've known him, he has never repaid a loan.

   a. Maybe Jim really is growing up. I should help him—with some money.

   b. Maybe Jim really is growing up. I should help him—with some words of encouragement and the offer to help out when needed.

   c. Maybe Jim really is growi...Oh, come on, who are we kidding?

3. Your sweetie has been working late for a few weeks, never getting home until the cock crows. He (or she) is beginning to look bedraggled.

   a. My poor darling needs to stand up to the boss and demand reasonable hours.

   b. I am getting a little annoyed with watching the late show alone while Sweetie burns the midnight oil. Hmmmm...burns...hot? How hot?

   c. I knew it, I just knew it. Where is that private detective's phone number?

4. You've been laboring on a ton of projects at work, and your boss tells you she is letting the folks in the corner offices know how truly brilliant you are.

   a. My long hours and overcrowded schedule are a fast trip to the top floor.

   b. I want to excel, so I really don't mind working long and hard. I'm beginning to wonder if she is being completely candid, though.

   c. Enough is enough. I bet she's taking credit for my work.

Suspicious Mind? Why Do You Ask?

5. Our national economy is chaotic and unstable lately.

   a. This is an international trend, and we will all have to work to be more financially responsible.

   b. Mistakes were made, and we need to be more watchful of national economic policy.

   c. I know exactly what happened. This was no accident; it was a well-planned tactic by....

6. You go into an upscale department store and browse through the fragrances. The clerk tells you that "Ode to Sinful Sensuality" is definitely you. You think:

   a. I must exude sensuality! Cool!

   b. I wonder what makes her think that's me? Maybe she's right...or maybe she just wants to make a sale.

   c. She's making fun of me. I certainly won't be buying anything here.

7. When you get home you hear your sweetie talking on the phone. Sweetie hangs up and doesn't mention the phone call.

   a. It's nice to be home after a long day. What should we do for dinner?

   b. Hmmm, should I take a peek at the caller ID? Nah, I'll just ask who was on the phone.

   c. As soon as I have some privacy I'm going to check caller ID and call the number to see who answers.

8. The movie you most closely relate to is:

   a. *It's a Wonderful Life* (sentimental and idealistic)

   b. *Apollo 13* (realistic but upbeat)

   c. *The Godfather* (cynical and bloodthirsty)

Suspicious Mind? Why Do You Ask?

9. You are sitting in a charming French restaurant waiting for a business acquaintance to join you. To pass the time, you are checking out the other diners.

   a. It looks like everyone is enjoying their meal. I'll look over the menu again while I wait for my dinner partner so I can order something special.

   b. My stomach is growling—when will this guy get here? He must not be particularly concerned about making me wait.

   c. I can't believe this guy's nerve. He set the time for the meeting, and he isn't even here. Everyone is looking at me wondering why I'm sitting here alone.

10. You are sitting at your desk working on a massive new project and you notice John and Nancy at the coffee station, chatting and chuckling.

   a. I wish I weren't wrapped in a tight deadline. I'd love to get a jolt of caffeine and join the chat.

   b. This doesn't seem fair. I'm slaving away over here while they have time for an extra-long break. Oh well, back to work.

   c. I saw John look over this way. They're laughing because I'm stuck at my desk doing their work.

Scoring

More "a" answers
Happily Trusting

You expect people to be trustworthy and honest, and, for the most part, you are correct. Expectations can create reality, and your reality is that the world is popu-

lated by folks who are basically decent, hardworking, and harmless. Your career may be in elementary education, religion, or the humanities. Every once in a while you are disappointed, but you have not allowed that to make you cynical or bitter.

Suspicious Mind? Why Do You Ask?

More "b" answers
Wary Realist

You are not as happily trusting as the first group, but you probably don't think people are out to get you, either. You  view your peers as neither beguilingly benevolent nor thoroughly bad lots. They are self-serving and competitive without being intentionally harmful (well, there are exceptions). You are likely to be working in finance, law enforcement, or health care. You simply believe in being wary and not standing in front of a target with circles painted on it.

More "c" answers
Disenchanted Idealist

You've been around, and you may think you've seen it all. The "all" has not always been pleasant, and you may be disappointed in humanity. Down deep in your soul you would probably adore being in the "a" group, but in your opinion the "a" people are easily led, uninformed, and dismally unrealistic. You may work in academia, the media, or politics. A deceitful and self-serving world is certainly not gratifying or laudable—nonetheless, what is, is.

what's that?
what are you talking about?

Paranoia is on the rise—at least it is in London and New York City, according to recent research. In good news for New Yorkers, this disturbing upward trend is more pronounced in London, especially among subway travelers. Or is it?

How Well Do You Cope with Disappointment?

If a disappointing situation is worrying you, you have been presented with an opportunity to cope. Coping can be relatively easy, once you get the hang of it. Healthy coping involves seeing a roadblock, acknowledging it, and developing a reasonably prudent plan to go over or around it—although on occasion you would be well advised to judiciously turn yourself around and find another road.

Individuals with good coping skills are generally able to resolve problems smoothly and maintain their relationships. Poor coping skills add more stress to already tense situations, and you may begin to feel overwhelmed. Many problems begin as poor solutions to other problems. So if you find yourself in a hole—stop digging, and take some time to evaluate your situation.

> **"One's best success comes after their greatest disappointments."**
> —*Henry Ward Beecher*

Of course, you can take the Dirty Harry route, if you have nerves of steel and a predisposition to misanthropy. Harry copes by blustering and squinting his way through life. Aggression is one way of coping, however it carries its own challenges—dead ends and unexpected cliffs. Aggressive individuals get through life, but they normally do it alone.

How Well Do You Cope with Disappointment?

Can you roll with the punches?

On a scale of 1 to 5, with 1 being the least like you and 5 being the most, how much do the responses to the following situations reflect your attitude?

1. You have come to the turbulent end of a legendary romance. You sniffle a good bit, run through a box of tissues, call your friends for support, and get back into the real world—wounded, but wiser.

   1   2   3   4   5

2. You just lost your job. "Oh my gosh—how am I going to pay my bills?" runs through your mind about a million times in a continuous loop. Then you pull up your bootstraps, tighten your belt, and start job hunting. You might find a better job.

   1   2   3   4   5

3. At your scheduled yearly physical you discover you are diabetic and must change your lifestyle. Naturally, you are thrown off-balance. Once the news sinks in, you read everything you can find on the disorder and question friends who are also diabetic.

   1   2   3   4   5

4. You are giving a presentation in front of an audience of executives when you notice several people snickering and pointing. You realize that your zipper is at half-mast. You turn around, zip up, and continue to speak—after all, you have important points to make.

   1   2   3   4   5

5. You have been stressed out by your heavy workload. You decide that this must stop! You buy some new walking shoes and begin to walk for 30 minutes each day, even if the work has to wait.

   1   2   3   4   5

How Well Do You Cope with Disappointment?

6. You hear through the grapevine that your lover may be spreading his or her love among the masses. Instead of grabbing your cell, hitting speed dial, and spewing forth every colorful name you can think of, you take a deep breath and decide to wait until later to address it—the grapevine isn't always right.   1   2   3   4   5

7. Your weight is creeping up, and you are distressed. You look up a few diet plans online and research which would be best for your lifestyle. In the meantime, you make yourself a small but healthy breakfast and grab a banana and a yogurt for a midmorning snack.   1   2   3   4   5

8. Your best friend is moving to another state. This is a real bummer! You cannot imagine what life will be like without your friend's companionship. After talking with a few people you trust, you begin looking on the bright side.   1   2   3   4   5

9. You are angry with a coworker who delights in spreading nasty innuendo to anyone who wanders by. You are the target this time. You take a few deep breaths and decide: "It isn't fair and I am seriously ticked, but I can't control her behavior."   1   2   3   4   5

10. You have identified and practice at least five successful ways to calm yourself when you are disappointed by life events.   1   2   3   4   5

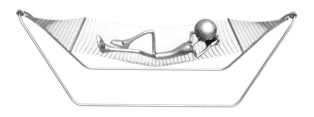

How Well Do You Cope with Disappointment?

Scoring

Add up the total number of points you circled in each scenario.

10–25 points
Coping Trainee

You may not be coping as successfully as you would like. Perhaps you feel overwhelmed and anxious at times. Researching and developing new coping strategies will have you coping like a pro in no time. Disappointments are normal; coping well is a skill. You can begin your chill campaign by reading the explanation at the beginning of this quiz—also, see page 145 for tips on coping with stress.

26–40 points
Coping Leader

You are coping well with common disappointments, however it's likely there are still times you would rather pull the covers over your head and take a break. Okay, go ahead and take a break, then return to strategizing about how to face the latest challenge with renewed energy. Expecting too much change too fast is discouraging, and this can turn into a vicious cycle Take your time.

41–50 points
Coping Master

You excel in coping strategies and problem solving. Your friends probably have your phone number on speed dial. They look to you when they find themselves in the proverbial "hot water." They know they can count on you for both wisdom *and* common sense. You are probably a cognitive thinker with a touch of "out of the box" thinking. Therefore, handling annoying disappointments may come quite naturally to you.

Are You Self-Confident?

Self-confidence is the little voice that says, "Go for it. You can do it!" even when all the world says, "Are you nuts?"

Not everyone is born with self-confidence. More often than not, it grows one success at a time. The question is, if you're not self-confident, how can you be successful? And if you're not successful, how can you feel self-confident? Like many things, this is a circular relationship.

To achieve success *and* robust self-confidence, follow these steps:

1. Believe in yourself.

2. Set realistic yet challenging goals.

3. Consistently move toward your goals. (Even minuscule steps count.)

> **"The person who says it cannot be done should not interrupt the person doing it."**
>
> —*Chinese Proverb*

If you want to touch the stars, you will need to make your dream tangible. What would it take to make you feel triumphant and self-confident? How will you know when you have arrived? Unless you claim each personal victory—small and large—your self-confidence won't increase, no matter how brilliant, talented, or attractive you happen to be. Your successes may be as seemingly unexceptional as your next indulgent massage, your next good hair day, or your next exhilarating date. Embrace them, and enjoy the glow of success!

Are You Self-Confident?

How much self-confidence do you have?

Mark the degree to which you agree or disagree
with the following statements.

	Strongly agree	**Agree**	**Strongly disagree**
1. I often feel self-conscious for no obvious reason.	❏	❏	❏
2. Sometimes I wonder what my friends and coworkers are thinking about me.	❏	❏	❏
3. I have doubts when I set a goal for myself.	❏	❏	❏
4. If someone asks me to break out of my comfort zone, I feel fearful.	❏	❏	❏
5. When I am having a conversation with someone, I evaluate everything I say while the words are coming out of my mouth.	❏	❏	❏
6. I really want people to like me, and sometimes I find myself acting like someone I'm not.	❏	❏	❏
7. I don't consider myself a cheerful person.	❏	❏	❏
8. If I am at a restaurant and my order is messed up, I don't say anything. I'd rather just eat what I am served.	❏	❏	❏

Are You Self-Confident?

	Strongly agree	Agree	Strongly disagree
9. I want to speak up at meetings and express my views, but I just can't seem to do it.	☐	☐	☐
10. I hate it when people look over my shoulder at my work.	☐	☐	☐
11. I seem to always be saying "I'm sorry."	☐	☐	☐
12. I would rather be drawn and quartered than make a presentation in public.	☐	☐	☐

Scoring

Give yourself **1 point** for "Strongly agree," **2 points** for "Agree," and **3 points** for "Strongly disagree."

12–18 points
Doubtful

You have doubts about wearing an "I am so fabulous" pin. Please, think back over the past week. How many successes did you have in that seven-day period? (A success is defined as *any* step toward *any* goal.) Now is a good time to define your goals, no matter how small. For example, your goal can be as small as making sure you leave for work early enough to stop for coffee. You might also want to define a few steps you can take toward achieving your goal. You may choose to set your alarm to go off ten minutes earlier, or you might decide to lay out your clothes the night before. Even though these steps on their own may not seem like much, your self-confidence may surge when you see just how much you accomplish—unnoticed. By the way, you may want to consider spending more time with optimistic, self-confident folks: Self-confidence can be contagious.

Are You Self-Confident?

19–25 points
Growing

You are a middle-of-the-road, "show me" type of individual. The middle of the road is a very comfortable place to be, isn't it? Since the mean is so darn comfortable, it may be tempting to resist moving forward. However, if you should decide to ratchet up your self-confidence a notch or two, start by rereading the quiz. Which statements did you mark as "agree" or "strongly agree"? Ask yourself, "How would my life be different if I strongly disagreed with that statement? Would it be better?" If you challenge yourself to change your mindset in one or more of these categories, you'll begin to notice a change. Notice that the heading to your scoring group is "Growing": Change is absolutely going to happen.

26–36 points
Enlightened

To whom do you owe your positive attitude? Why not call him or her right now and say, "Thank you so much"? You trust yourself because of a positive attitude and a long line of successes, and obviously you've been doing the right things. But...(isn't there always a "but"?) be sure you read the sidebar (below), because there really can be too much of a good thing. True confidence is gentle and kind—and helpful.

mirror, mirror, on the wall...

A **narcissist** is someone who believes that he or she is the center of the universe. Anyone who disagrees with a narcissist's self-love will be dismissed and replaced with someone who admires the narcissist's extraordinary individuality—at least for the time being. As one might imagine, narcissists are constantly in need of new admirers and don't tend to be loyal friends—they're too involved with themselves to pay much attention to others.

Are You the Ultimate Optimist?

Life is outrageously entertaining for eternal optimists. They tend to dance to the beat of a different drummer, and they thoroughly enjoy the dance. For them, the sun is always shining, the bread always rises, and they meet the coolest people wherever they go. Optimists are happy in their beautifully blissful world.

Are you as optimistic as famous hopeful thinkers Helen Keller and Winston Churchill? Can you be as upbeat as the unstoppable Forrest Gump or the melodious and cheerful Little Orphan Annie? If so, studies show you will live longer, love better, enjoy more robust health, and achieve triumphs impossible for the mistrustful and pessimistic.

> **An optimist travels from nowhere with nothing to happiness.**
> —*Mark Twain*

> **For myself I am an optimist—it does not seem to be much use being anything else.**
> —*Winston Churchill*

> **No pessimist ever discovered the secret of the stars.**
> —*Helen Keller*

Are You the Ultimate Optimist?

Is your glass half full or half empty?

Choose the response that is most like your life philosophy.

1. You just walked into a party crowded with strangers. Your first thought is:

   a. This is a good opportunity to meet new people.

   b. I don't see a familiar face anywhere. If I back out slowly, maybe no one will notice.

   c. Yikes, I'm underdressed.

2. You have just completed a leadership test for a coveted promotion at work. You think:

   a. That was fun! I bet I'll hear great news tomorrow.

   b. I can't believe I blew the test. What a mess! They'll probably decide I'm not even qualified for the job I have now.

   c. Drat, I messed up! I am going to head home, pop in a DVD, and try to forget about today.

3. You and your sweetie had a terrible argument and he (she) walked out the door, saying, "Frankly, my dear, I don't...." Your first thought is:

   a. Couples have arguments. After we cool off, I'm sure we'll work it out.

   b. This is it; we're through. There is nothing I can do now.

   c. This isn't the first time we have clashed, but I think it was worse than ever before.

4. A stranger at a party smiles at you and compliments you on your gorgeous eyes. You think:

   a. That's very sweet. My eyes *are* my best feature.

   b. I guess my hair looks awful and these pants make me look fat. Why else would someone mention my eyes unless they were searching for something nice to say?

   c. Hmmm, I suppose my eyes are pretty nice. This shirt must bring out the color in them.

Are You the Ultimate Optimist?

5. The housing market is in a slump. Your best friend says she is buying a house while home prices and interest rates are at remarkable lows. You think:

   a. What a great idea! I'm going to contact a mortgage broker today.

   b. She's crazy! The entire economy could collapse any day now.

   c. She may be right, but then again, she may be wrong. I don't know what to do.

6. Your boss has asked you to take on a new project that could propel you to the dizzying heights of middle management—if you succeed. Your first thought is:

   a. This is a fabulous opportunity to shine!

   b. This could be a disaster if I fail. In fact, it probably *will* be a disaster.

   c. Maybe this could work out if I am exceptionally lucky.

7. Your life philosophy is:

   a. Life is soooo exciting! I can hardly wait for tomorrow.

   b. Life is tough, and then you die.

   c. Life can be maneuvered if one is lucky and exceptionally careful.

8. You just won $10,000 in a contest. You think:

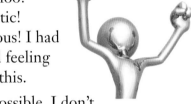

   a. Woo-hoo! Fantastic! Fabulous! I had a good feeling about this.

   b. Not possible. I don't enter contests. Waste of time.

   c. Cool. But rats, now I'll have to pay the government more than a third in taxes.

9. Your friends want to introduce you to a "very special person with a great personality." Your first thought is:

   a. Fun! My friends are always looking out for me.

   b. "Great personality?" We all know what that means. No, thank you.

   c. Oh, all right, but I won't get my hopes up.

Are You the Ultimate Optimist?

10. You are scheduled to a take two week vacation from work. Your company stresses the need for relaxation and leisure time. You think:

a. Terrific! I've been dying to take a cruise! Crystal-clear water, fabulous food, exotic ports, and exciting new people—my kind of adventure.

b. Ugh. I don't have the money to go anywhere, and even if I did, who would water my plants and take in the mail?

c. Vacation? Okay, I'll go; I guess I could use a break.

Scoring

More "a" answers

The Eternal Optimist

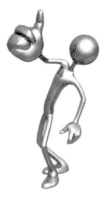

You are blissfully optimistic and delighted with your life. You see your future as full of surprises and opportunities. You probably have a good sense of humor and enjoy people, even if they are not perfect.

The funny thing about optimism is that people want to live up to your optimistic perception of them. We all need optimists to help us to be our best.

when getting mad can make you happy

One sign of a truly optimist person is the ability to express righteous anger. "Anger" and "optimism" may sound contradictory, but a recent study indicates that anger is more likely to lead to optimism, whereas fear leads to pessimism. Optimists have learned to trust their emotions because of a positive attitude and a long line of successes.

Are You an Optimist?

More "b" answers
The Pessimist

You have had a trying year, haven't you? It looks like you're dreadfully low on optimism, or maybe you are in the middle of a mood downswing due to a distressing situation. If you are normally more buoyant, then this bleakness will probably pass and you will be your old lighthearted self again. If your friends hint that you are not exactly the life of the party, perhaps you need to find some optimistic folks to hang out with. The best thing you can do is surround yourself with happy people; your differences will be noticeable, and you'll probably be inspired to turn to the light.

More "c" answers
The Middle Ground

You're no Orphan Annie, but you aren't all gloom and doom like *Jane Eyre's* Edward Rochester either. Some people would call you a realist, in that you see "real" life unembellished by gloominess or an overly cheerful nature. They may be right. However, since it is healthier to be optimistic, it's a good idea to try to lean in that direction. If you feel yourself tipping toward the dark side, close your eyes and think about Little Orphan Annie. She's right, you know: The sun *will* come out tomorrow.

Everyone Else

If you are all over the board with your answers, perhaps you are still writing your life philosophy and haven't yet settled on something that is comfortable for you. Hint: Aim for the optimistic; it's in your best interest. Studies have shown that optimists are generally healthier and enjoy greater longevity than pessimists; they are generally better equipped to deal with stress; and they have great potential for achievement in life.

CHAPTER 7

JUST FOR FUN

Life can turn serious on us—that is why we need to have serious fun—often. This chapter will point you in the right direction.

You'll learn more about your sensuality—do you luxuriate in your five senses, or are you more influenced by rationality than sensuality? Some people think the world is composed of two types of people: canine and feline. Are you a protective, devoted dog or a cunning or rascally cat?

Are you superstitious? The pursuit of lucky four-leaf clovers seems to be in our blood. Take the quiz and learn more about your superstitious beliefs. Are you a Harry Potter fan? Even if you've never cracked open a cover or seen one of the movies, you can get lost in the adventure with this interesting quiz. And speaking of wizards and magic…Do you have a spine-tingling interest in the supernatural?

As you take the quizzes in this chapter, remember: Fun is your only goal—go for it!

Sensual or Sensible?

Are you captivated by the breeze from the subway, the luscious whipped cream on your latte, and the velvety texture of your favorite jacket? Sensuality is the ability to enjoy—even more, to luxuriate in—the tantalizing vibes from all of your senses. This delight in the senses is separate from economy, function, and logic; it is purely, well—sensual.

> **"Oh, do you feel the breeze from the subway? Isn't it delicious?"**
>
> —*Marilyn Monroe,* The Seven Year Itch

You will find sensual people sniffing pricy, pungent perfumes; indulging in dark, creamy cocoa; and soaking in balmy, bubbly baths, perhaps while sipping a little bubbly to tickle the nose and please the palate.

You may wonder if such indulgences are sinfully over the top. No, they're not. Allowing these little luxuries makes life more stimulating.

Do you indulge your senses?

Which answer more closely matches your preferences?

1. You are shopping at a cute little boutique, and you must choose between a slinky black velvet skirt or a sensible wool cap. You have no occasion to which to wear the dress, and it has been a cold winter so far....

    a. Who could resist the romantic drape and sultry touch of velvet on their skin?

    b. It's cold outside—wrap up the wool cap, please.

2. You're in the market for a new house, and you must choose between one with granite countertops or one with a fireplace.

    a. Granite lasts forever, and it will increase the resale value of the home.

    b. I can just see myself lounging in front of the fire, enjoying the toasty feel, the aroma of fresh-cut wood, and the warm glow.

Sensual or Sensible?

3. Your main squeeze has taken you to the hottest restaurant in town. As the waiter fawns over you, he suggests dessert. The specials tonight are a gooey dark chocolate and black cherry cake with crème fraiche or an organic tofu with a rare Mongolian berry topping.

a. Chocolate? Did you say dark and gooey? Extra napkins, please!

b. Mongolian berries, tofu…sounds healthy. What a refreshing way to top off the meal.

4. You need a new pair of pajamas, and two different styles are on sale: a nice, long-wearing, heavy cotton in sensible taupe, and a soft pink pair in the fluffiest, most highly touchable fleece.

a. The taupe pair looks warm and comfortable, and it'll last forever. And look how affordable it is!

b. Mmm-mmm, fleece. Combine that with my 600-thread-count sheets and feather-down comforter, and I may never get out of bed.

5. You are going out on a first date, and you are trying to decide what to wear.

a. No doubt about it, the cashmere sweater says "I'm touchable."

b. That nice rayon suit fits well, and it never wrinkles. Yes, that will do quite nicely.

6. You are considering trading in your car while prices and interest rates are low. You've got your eye on two in particular: an economical sedan that'll really save you a bunch on gas, and a preowned, sexy, sleek, red convertible.

a. With the sedan I could cut my gas bill in half, and look at the size of that trunk! That'll hold two weeks of groceries and more.

b. I was born to own a convertible. I can already feel the wind in my hair and the sun beating down on my shoulders.

Sensual or Sensible?

7. William Congreve said: "Music has charms to soothe the savage beast." What type of music charms and soothes you?

   a. Stirring, melodious jazz; whisky-smooth soul; soft rock; and/or calming classic strings.

   b. Hand-clapping, foot-tapping drumbeats; wild guitar riffs; heavy metal rock; and/or fast, loud rap.

8. You're lucky enough to have room for a small garden. How will you indulge your inner landscape architect?

   a. A tomato plant would be convenient for salads. Perhaps a broccoli plant or two; they are loaded with healthful vitamins.

   b. An abundance of lush, flowering plants and greenery, including a fragrant miniature rose bush, aromatic rosemary and mint, a velvety soft lambs' ear plant, and a gorgeous, unexpected night-blooming cereus, all under the gentle umbrella of a graceful magnolia tree.

9. Which of the following accessories are more commonly found in your home?

   a. Scented candles and fresh-cut flowers are everywhere. The candles shimmer and cast an enticing aroma throughout the whole house.

   b. I leave a dependable flashlight in every room, in case the electricity suddenly decides to malfunction.

10. You will be making a PowerPoint presentation at work next week, unveiling the huge project you have been working on for weeks. You want to make a lasting impression.

    a. A simple, neat presentation will keep things relevant and understandable. Note to self: Pick up gray suit from cleaners.

    b. Color and imagery will grab their attention, and I'll also throw in some emotional words (*win, triumph, enhance, empower*). Note to self: Wear colorful, friendly materials and a subtle fragrance. Colors should be powerful, but not over the top.

Sensual or Sensible?

Scoring

For all odd-numbered questions, give yourself **1 point** if you answered "a." For the even-numbered questions, give yourself **1 point** for each "b" answer.

0–3 points
More Sense than Sensibility

You appear to be more influenced by rationality than sensuality. Maybe pure logic is working for you—if it is, great! We all need some indulgences in life, so make sure you take time to stop and smell the roses. If you sizzle (or simmer) in the romance department and feel pampered, by all means, continue doing what you're doing. If, on the other hand, you feel your life is missing some gusto, try adding some warm and fuzzy (or soft and silky). Start by reviewing some of the quiz questions, and see what you can do to flip some of your answers to the softer side.

4–7 points
Quite Sensual

We are all sensual creatures, but sensuality is a matter of degree. It's clear you exhibit a strong dose of sensual inclination; perhaps you enjoy a warm aromatic bath and love soothing music. You are definitely developing the sensuous you. If you want to send your sensuality score soaring even higher, stop and smell a few more roses, enjoy the taste of something decadent, or pamper yourself with the feel of something luxurious.

8–10 points
Exquisitely Sensual

You are an expert at indulging your senses. Your cup brims over with sumptuous, rich, and heady sensations. Your friends watch you explore—touching, observing, tasting, drinking in your world. They love to bask in your warm, soft light. Don't hide your love of the sensory pleasures. Freely share your secrets. Everyone deserves a generous slice of sensuous opulence in his or her life. Just remember not to throw practicality out the window—there's something to be said for having a warm cap in wintertime and a car that's roomy enough for your day-to-day lifestyle.

Do You Have a Feline Purrrr-sonality?

Some people think the world is composed of two types of people: feline and canine. We all have our preference, and we're all certain that our preference is the correct one: either the majestic cat or the dearly loved dog. Many people believe that human personalities mesh well with one or the other. Perhaps that explains our devotion to our choice—we share characteristics with them. (You may also want to check out the Canine Personality quiz on page 177.)

The feline personality is quite distinctive: stealthy, cunning, purrrr-fectly adorable. And there's more than one type of cat, of course. Do you share characteristics with the sophisticated, regal descendents of the awesome saber-toothed tiger? Or are you, purr-chance, right at home perched on a window seat watching the Tweety birds?

> **"After scolding one's cat one looks into its face and is seized by the ugly suspicion that it understood every word. And has filed it for reference."**
>
> —*Charlotte Gray*

Do You Have a Feline Purrrr-sonality?

are you the cat's meow?

Choose the most fitting answer for each question—or does the cat have your tongue?

1. When I take in a movie, I like to:

   a. Head to the neighborhood theater for an indie film.

   b. Pop out to see the latest action/ adventure extravaganza.

2. My morning routine is:

   a. A quick shower and a comb through my hair—if I remember.

   b. A nice, long bubble bath and a deep-conditioning treatment.

3. My style of communication is:

   a. I have a couple of close friends I enjoy talking to; otherwise I'll sit back and listen (or not).

   b. I tell it all: I'm forthcoming, warm, and gregarious.

4. I prefer:

   a. Helping or guiding others.

   b. Investigating, analyzing, or accumulating knowledge.

5. My body movement is:

   a. Bold, stealthy, athletic, or silent.

   b. Tentative, lackadaisical, or adorably uncoordinated.

6. I am likely to:

   a. Forgive and forget.

   b. Quietly note grievances and file for future reference.

7. When it comes to other people:

   a. I notice everything and use that information to make decisions about others.

   b. I am gregarious and optimistic, and I expect the best from most people—and I usually get it.

8. My general appearance is:

   a. Tousled and casual.

   b. Aloof and dignified.

9. This song could have been written about me:

   a. "I Did It My Way"

   b. "What a Wonderful World"

10. When it comes to food, I prefer:

   a. Rare roast beef, a mouthwatering cheeseburger, or rack of lamb.

   b. Tofu, an egg-white omelette, and steamed veggies.

Do You Have a Feline Purrrr-sonality?

Scoring

Odd-numbered questions: Give yourself **1 point** for each "a" answer. Even-numbered questions: Give yourself **1 point** for each "b" answer.

0–3 points
The Cat's Away
Well, well...look what the cat *didn't* drag in. Your defining characteristics are outgoing, casual, and optimistic: Though you are probably a very keen observer, your perception of life and humanity is more thoughtful and generous than that of the average Persian. You are a team player willing to do your part, no matter what that happens to be. People come to you to cry on your shoulder and to have their hand held. You tend to have a patient ear and a calm, soothing way of speaking.

You are not a cat after all, but that's okay: You are helpful, laid-back, loyal, and genial—no one's purr-fect.

4–7 points
Here, Kitty, Kitty
You have some feline qualities. You are willing and able to go forth alone and lead anyone who needs to be led, as long as they are willing to follow. However, you don't actively seek the role—it must be thrust upon you. (You have this in common with George Washington, so you're in good company.)

You value appearance, but you do not live for good hair days. Hairballs are not a big problem; in fact, your hair may not be your crowning glory. You are optimistic by nature, but you have also learned a few hard truths along the way. You might best be called a realist who pines to be an optimist.

8–10 points
The Cat's Out of the Bag
What's up, pussycat? You are independent, a natural leader (when you feel inclined to lead), and you certainly don't follow. You are a Napoleon, an Alexander the Great, when the mood strikes you. You are superbly fastidious—especially about your appearance. You may groom yourself more for the sheer pleasure it brings you than to please anyone else.

You can be unpredictable, changing at the drop of a catnip treat. You are a loyal, though mildly temperamental, friend to the select people you count as true friends. Meow!

176

Do You Have a Canine Personality?

S ure, we've heard all the doggy clichés: A dog is man's best friend. A barking dog never bites. Let sleeping dogs lie. You can't teach an old dog new tricks. Even though these words are all about dogs, read closer and you'll see they contain valuable lessons for humans as well.

More than two centuries ago, the great poet Lord Byron eulogized a beloved Newfoundland dog with these words: "Beauty without Vanity, Strength without Insolence, Courage without Ferocity, and all the Virtues of Man, without his Vices."

Now, what human could live up to this description? Indeed, Byron went on to say, "This Praise . . . would be unmeaning flattery if inscribed over human ashes."

Why do we praise the virtue of a dog well beyond our more guarded appraisal of human virtue? Dogs are described as loyal, courageous, fun-loving, accepting, warm-hearted . . . and the list goes on. As you consider your own personality characteristics and compare them to that of our canine companions, perhaps you will feel a touch of flattering kinship.

> **"I think dogs are the most amazing creatures; they give unconditional love. For me they are the role model for being alive."**
>
> —*Gilda Radner*

Do You Have a Canine Personality?

Do you have puppy power?

Put a checkmark in the box that best describes you: **Growl** *(no way)*, **Whimper** *(maybe)*, or **Wag, wag** *(yeah, yeah!)*.

	Growl	Whimper	Wag, Wag
1. I drop what I am doing and listen to my friends when one needs a sympathetic ear.	☐	☐	☐
2. I have a well-earned reputation among my friends for my fierce loyalty.	☐	☐	☐
3. I can be trusted to be myself in public without pretense or affectation—what you see is what you get.	☐	☐	☐
4. I am relatively grounded and stable; you won't see mood swings here.	☐	☐	☐
5. I can be counted on to protect my friends and family when the wolf is at the door.	☐	☐	☐
6. Really, I'm pretty cool with an upbeat attitude—just throw a ball and watch me go.	☐	☐	☐
7. I am without prejudice or bias: I accept everyone as good folks until I have ample reason to grab a pant leg.	☐	☐	☐
8. I love the great outdoors, exercise, and hanging out with my buds.	☐	☐	☐
9. I love to get attention from my favorite folks, but I understand that I'm not the center of the universe.	☐	☐	☐
10. Sure, grooming is cool, but I don't spend my life panting in front of a mirror.	☐	☐	☐

Do You Have a Canine Personality?

Scoring

Give yourself **1 point** for each "Growl," **2 points** for each "Whimper," and **3 points** for each "Wag, wag."

10–15 points
You're Barking Up the Wrong Tree

Rin Tin Tin you are not. You are more aloof than a typical canine—an intellectual, or maybe you just like to do your own thing. Your appearance may be quite important to you; if so, you probably fully understand the meaning of "you only have one chance to make a good first impression." You are cunningly perceptive, and you're no one's toy to be manipulated or doormat to be used.

Robust self-confidence is essential (take our self-confidence quiz on page 160) if you hope to make your mark on the world. Luckily, your profile suggests that you are quite confident and capable.

16–23 points
Every Dog Has Its Day

You are gifted with many diverse attributes. You are adaptable and resilient, in that you can call on the characteristics that work best for you in any situation. You are "the fit" in "survival of the fittest." You are probably proficient in a number of areas and cannot be pinned down by the usual labels: cognitive, risk taker, or introverted/extroverted. Your friends may have decided that you are charmingly unpredictable. You aren't unpredictable; you are an intriguing, unique breed.

24–30 points
Hot Dog!

Loyal and *affectionate* probably best describe your personality type. You share qualities with the tenacious bulldog, the winsome Irish setter, the playful Labrador retriever—even the daring and protective German shepherd. Your woof is your bond, and you can be trusted without reservation. Accepting and optimistic, you expect to find the best in human nature.

Socially, you probably have a wide circle of friends and acquaintances who have discovered, to their delight, that you can be counted on when the going gets rough. They also value your sympathetic nature, outdoorsy charm, and sense of humor.

Does Your Personality Embrace a Harry Potter Character?

Why do we love Harry Potter? People have always been fascinated by magic and drawn to heart-thumping adventure and vicarious risk-taking. Researchers suggest that many of us are attracted to men and women who are adventurous and perhaps even dangerous. (See our Risk Taker quiz on page 136.) It's in our genes.

The Harry Potter genre crosses over into a number of themes: fairy tale, action/adventure, fantasy, and mystery. Although fictional, the characters feel true to life. We can relate to Harry and his friends as they fight for truth, knowledge, and social justice. We can unite with them against the forces of evil. And we can rejoice with them as they celebrate friendship, love, and loyalty. Each of the characters has a unique personality. With whom do you identify most?

> **"Magic is believing in yourself. If you can do that, you can make anything happen."**
>
> —*Goethe*

Does Your Personality Embrace a Harry Potter Character?

Which character would you transfigure into?

1. When you hear the name "Harry Potter," what comes to your mind first?

   a. His haunting loss—the death of his parents

   b. His loyalty to his friends

   c. His magic spells

   d. His hair-raising adventures

2. What is your favorite spell?

   a. *Expelliarmus* (disarms other wizards)

   b. *Legilimens* (used to delve into the minds of others and learn their private thoughts)

   c. *Fidelius Charm* (a charm involving the revelation of secret information stored within someone's soul)

   d. *Mobilicorpus* (used to levitate and move around troublesome wizards)

3. What is your dominant emotion when you read the Harry Potter books or watch the movies?

   a. Melancholy

   b. Curiosity

   c. Interest

   d. Excitement

4. At which location did you feel most emotionally involved in the story?

   a. The Burrow (the Weasleys' house)

   b. Hogwarts library (Restricted section)

   c. The Ministry of Magic

   d. The Forbidden Forest

5. Which event is most appealing to you?

   a. A Quidditch match

   b. The O.W.L. or N.E.W.T. exams

   c. The House-Sorting Feast

   d. The Tri-Wizard Tournament

6. Which creature is most interesting to you?

   a. Hagrid's lovable, affectionate dog, Fang

   b. A highly intelligent Centaur, with the head and torso of a human and the body of a horse

   c. A Thestral, the winged horse-like creature that is invisible to those who have not witnessed death

   d. A Hippogriff, with the wings, claws, and head of a griffin and the body and hindquarters of a horse

Does Your Personality Embrace a Harry Potter Character?

7. For which Hogwarts class would you most likely sign up?

   a. Defense Against the Dark Arts

   b. History of Magic

   c. Ancient Runes

   d. Transfiguration

8. If you looked into a magical mirror that could grant your heart's desire, what would you see?

   a. A safe life for the people I love

   b. Universal health care and equal rights for all

   c. The secrets of the universe

   d. A life of adventure

9. If you were to use a secret curse to turn someone into a toad, it would probably be:

   a. Dudley Dursley

   b. Ron, when he's being particularly bothersome

   c. Aberforth Dumbledore (Professor Dumbledore's younger brother)

   d. Severus Snape

10. To which of the following characters do you feel most connected?

   a. Harry Potter

   b. Hermione Granger

   c. Albus Dumbledore

   d. Sirius Black

Scoring

More "a" answers
Reluctant Hero

Like **Harry**, you see the pathos in life and feel it deeply. You are likely to focus on the inequities in life and strive to make the world a better place for all of us. The world needs your profile type to help us remember what we "should" be doing. You likely work in the humanities or for a not-for-profit organization—doing your part to save the world. Make sure to take some time to enjoy your life without feel-ing responsible for anything other than laughing, eating great food, and hanging out with your buddies. (Why not go see a Harry Potter movie on a night out with friends?)

More "b" answers
Problem Solver

You and **Hermione** both notice the ineq-uities in life, but you realize that there is only so much you can do, and you likely have an enviable balance in your life. You

Does Your Personality Embrace a Harry Potter Character?

are driven to succeed; indeed, you may occasionally have to pull back in your quest to overachieve. With your quick wit and loyalty, you are a delight to your friends and family—you always seem to know what to do to make their lives feel stable and fun.

More "c" answers
Wise Mentor

You channel **Professor Dumbledore** in the way you wonder about things: what makes them tick, how to put them together, and what it all means. You are the scientist, observer, recorder of information. A good job match for you would likely be in the field of science, math, communications, intelligence, teaching, or journalism. As a "scientist," you are probably able to stand back, restrain your emotions, and see situations from an objective perspective. Your friends admire you because you always have something new and interesting to share with them—and you will tell them the truth.

More "d" answers
Bold Adventurer

You, like Harry's godfather **Sirius Black**, are into drama, adventure, warriors, and wherever the exciting journey happens to take you. You may live vicariously through action/adventure books, movies, and, perhaps, games. You may also bring this zest for excitement into your "real" life. If so, enjoy the drama without taking too many unnecessary risks. Your career may be  anything from police officer to paleontologist depending on how much your quest for danger extends to the real world. Keep those medical premiums up to date and your lucky charm in your pocket, and see our Risk Taker quiz on page 136.

fun fact

In the libraries of Great Britain, *Harry Potter and the Deathly Hallows* is the most borrowed book, though interestingly, it is not the most stolen book. (*London A–Z* is most often swiped.)

"Brilliant!"

Remember, no matter how dark things may seem, there is always a bright spot. As Harry would tell us, having Potions class last thing on Friday is a good thing, because it means Snape "won't have the time to poison us all!" Look for your personal magic, and use it to bring sparkle and fun to your life.

Do You Believe in Ghosts?

Are you sensitive to the shadowy realm? Used in this context, "sensitive" describes people who are open to possibilities beyond their five traditional senses. They are open to the spirit world and may be able to perceive a world that is heavily cloaked, invisible to their more skeptical brothers and sisters. Sensitive individuals are open to all explanations and only exclude an option once they have hard evidence that demonstrates, beyond a shadow of a doubt, that a possibility is purely imaginative.

> **From ghoulies and ghosties**
> **And long-leggedy beasties**
> **And things that go bump**
>   **in the night,**
> **Good Lord, deliver us!**
>
> —*Scottish saying*

who you gonna call?

As ghost hunter Scott Haddis says, people who are too willing to believe in ghosts "see" them in every flickering light and dark shadow, while the person who is completely close-minded would not see a ghost if it were beating on a drum and singing the national anthem. An unbiased, open mind appears to be the defining personality trait of a true ghost hunter.

Are you one of these exquisitely perceptive individuals? Are you able to believe in the ethereal realm of the supernatural?

If you are, you're not alone. More than 50 percent of Americans

Do You Believe in Ghosts?

will readily admit that they believe in ghosts. And it's well documented that some very well thought of, highly respected public figures believed in spirits beyond our sphere. The great Harry Houdini spent much of his life attempting to communicate with his dead mother—yet, sadly, never succeeded. Sherlock Holmes creator Sir Arthur Conan Doyle, whose beloved second wife was a medium, probably

contacted entirely too many suspiciously bogus "spirits." Abraham Lincoln, reputed to be a believer, is said to haunt the White House today—spooking visitors and guests when in a mischievous mood.

Do you believe in ghosts? Are you convinced beyond a shadow of a doubt that they exist among us? Or maybe you're open to the possibility and willing to be convinced, but you retain a robust skepticism.

Ghost story

1. Have you ever known the phone would ring and who was on the other end—before it rang?

   Yes   No

2. Have your friends told you they know you will listen to them without judging what they say?

   Yes   No

3. Do some of your friends believe in the supernatural?

   Yes   No

4. Do you read about (or view) a wide variety of topics, including science and atypical literature?

   Yes   No

Do You Believe in Ghosts?

5. Have you ever dreamed about something that later happened?

Yes   No

6. Have you ever perceived (i.e., heard, saw, felt, and/or sensed) something you believed might be a ghostly manifestation?

Yes   No

7. Normally, do you follow your own counsel rather than accepting the opinion of the crowd?

Yes   No

8. Are your decisions often based on your gut feelings rather than science or logic?

Yes   No

9. Are you self-confident and relatively immune to criticism?

Yes   No

10. Would be willing to join a ghost hunters group?

Yes   No

just because it goes bump in the night doesn't mean it's a ghost

Keep in mind that in the nebulous realm of specters, there are no easy answers. Be on the lookout for those who would enhance their status or bank account by bamboozling the unwary.

Scoring

Total your "yes" responses and give yourself **1 point** for each.

0–3 points
The Unbelieving
So you're not open to the unusual, bizarre, or spooky; you want to see the proof in the pudding. You have a more cognitive and dogmatic personality and you, no doubt, rely on scientific explanations for odd occurrences. You are likely to be in one of the cognitive professions: Science or math professor, surgeon, engineer, military leader, or strategist are a few of the occupations that might be appealing to the highly cognitive.

Do You Believe in Ghosts?

You would walk though a graveyard whistling at midnight. Or maybe, just maybe, you might admit to feeling just a little prickle on the back of your neck... wouldn't you?

4–7 points
The Unconvinced

You're probably willing to be convinced that something that goes bump in the night might not have an easy explanation. You are hovering over the paranormal, but you may change your mind at any moment and head for rock-solid ground. Maybe a little research on the paranormal would help you to make a decision, or perhaps you merely like to keep your options open. You have an open and intuitive mind.

You would walk through a graveyard at night without fear. At the same time,

you wouldn't be astounded to see something white and wispy hovering above an ancient marker...you just never know.

8–10 points
The Believers

You have at least eight personality characteristics and actual experiences that indicate your belief, no matter how tentative, in the paranormal. You have lots of company; if you begin asking friends and coworkers if they have ever had a paranormal experience you may be surprised at the number who say yes. Your career choice is likely to be in an artistic or emotive field, such as the humanities.

You would certainly walk through a graveyard at night—carrying your camera and an energy-seeking device.

Are You Superstitious?

Having superstitious beliefs is a very human trait. All societies have superstitions, some of which are useful and help to direct us away from dangerous or self-defeating behaviors. For example, have you ever heard that it is unlucky for three people to light their cigarettes on a single match? This superstition was born in World War I for good reason: Soldiers knew that it was dangerous to keep a flame lit for too long, because the light might alert the enemy to the location of their foxhole. As this rule of combat moved away from the context of war, it became a superstition that people began to follow without really understanding why. It's quite common for customs to live on as the explanations behind them are lost with the passage of time—turning the customs into superstitions.

"The root of all superstition is that [people] observe when a thing hits, but not when it misses."

—*Francis Bacon*

So why are we superstitious? For one thing, superstitions can momentarily reduce our anxiety if we believe that "magical" behaviors empower us—provide us with some control over the uncontrollable. If you believe something will be beneficial, such as wearing your lucky tie to a job interview, you will probably feel more confident and, therefore, act more confident. (Of course, if you don't get the job, you may abandon that superstition.) Well, you may or may not get that job, but one thing to keep in mind is

Are You Superstitious?

that you shouldn't let a superstitious belief interfere with "real" life—it's not a good idea to rely so much on your lucky tie that you neglect to prepare for the interview.

Studies have indicated that half of us are at least a little superstitious. According to the same studies, older individuals are less superstitious than younger, and men are less superstitious than women.

How superstitious are you?

1. Do you feel in control in most situations?

   Yes   No

2. Do you feel distinctly uncomfortable when a black cat runs in front of you?

   Yes   No

3. If you were boarding an airplane and you noticed that you would be in the 13th row, would you strongly consider asking for a different seat?

   Yes   No

4. Are you open-minded and willing to try all options?

   Yes   No

5. Do you have an object, such as a lucky pen, that makes you feel more confident and in control?

   Yes   No

Are You Superstitious?

6. Do you nod in understanding when someone you know exhibits superstitious behaviors?

Yes   No

7. Do you believe that luck is very important in reaching your goals?

Yes   No

8. Have you ever changed your plans because you had a nagging feeling that something wasn't right?

Yes   No

9. Have you ever had the disquieting "feeling" that you would never see a particular person again?

Yes   No

10. Do you avoid "tooting your own horn" because it might jinx your good fortune? (Or, if you do boast, do you make sure you knock three times on wood?)

Yes   No

11. If you were walking down the sidewalk and a ladder blocked your path, would you change your route to avoid it?

Yes   No

12. If you spilled salt, would you feel compelled to throw some over your shoulder?

Yes   No

13. Do you feel uncomfortable because this quiz has 13 questions?

Yes   No

Are You Superstitious?

Scoring

Give yourself **1 point** for each "yes" answer.

0–4 points
The Skeptic

You probably depend on your personal skills and ability to navigate your way through life. Perhaps you believe that you don't need luck to smooth your way. According to your quiz results, you appear to be virtually superstition-free. (Then again, you may have a couple of habits or beliefs that have not been swept away by skepticism and iron logic.)

Did Oscar Wilde speak for you when he said, "There is no such thing as an omen. Destiny does not send us heralds. She is too wise or too cruel for that."?

5–8 points
The Uncommitted

Sure, you have a few lucky charms, and you probably believe that good things come in threes, that horse-shoes bring good luck, 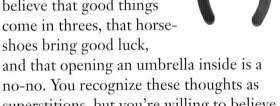 and that opening an umbrella inside is a no-no. You recognize these thoughts as superstitions, but you're willing to believe them—to a point. The difference between you and the skeptics in the first group is that you listen to your gut feelings more

often and are more apt to adjust your behavior accordingly—or at least consider it. You may notice little nuances that transform into intuition and gut feelings.

a sinking feeling

Did you know that several people who were scheduled to set sail on the *Titanic* reported uneasy feelings or premonitions strong enough to keep them from boarding the vessel? Records show that George and Edith Vanderbilt cancelled their passage on the advice of someone in their family, who warned them, "So many things can go wrong on a maiden voyage." Did these people just get lucky, or did fate step in?

9–13 points
The True Believer

You pay attention to your environment and to your beliefs. Your daily thoughts and feelings have probably played a significant part in helping you cope in life. No doubt you have a few lucky objects, a lucky outfit, and a routine you make sure

Are You Superstitious?

you follow. You're also careful to observe the rules of some common folk beliefs. You would never consider walking under a ladder or getting in the path of a black cat, and on Friday the 13th you'll keep a low profile, thank you very much. It generally doesn't hurt to indulge these superstitions, and as far as you're concerned, why take a chance? (Knock on wood.) Perhaps you'd be interested in learning the roots of some of these superstitions so you can see for yourself if they make sense.

common superstitions

Seeing an ambulance is unlucky unless you pinch your nose or hold your breath until you see a black or a brown dog.

If you blow out all the candles on your birthday cake with the first puff your wish will come true.

If you say good-bye to a friend on a bridge, you will never see each other again.

If a black cat walks toward you, it brings good fortune, but if it walks away, it takes the good luck with it.

It's bad luck to pick up a coin if it's tails side up. Good luck comes if it's heads up.

It's bad luck to leave a house through a different door than the one used to come into it.

Fingernail cuttings should be saved, burned, or buried.

You must hold your breath while going past a cemetery or you will breathe in the spirit of someone who has recently died.

It's bad luck to open an umbrella inside the house, especially if you put it over your head.

If you leave a rocking chair rocking when empty, it invites evil spirits to come into your house to sit in the rocking chair.

If you use the same pencil to take a test that you used while studying for the test, the pencil will remember the answers.